THE COMPLETE KEESHOND

The Complete

KEESHOND

by

Clementine Peterson

1980—Sixth Printing
HOWELL BOOK HOUSE INC.
230 Park Avenue
New York, N.Y. 10169

Contents

Drawings, pp. 13, 19, 154, 219, 229 and 249 are by Chris Blom
Silhouettes on title page by the author

Foreword

HERE is an engrossing chronicle of the Keeshond, written by one
of the enthusiasts most responsible for the breed's great growth and
impact today. Personal experiences and an unbounded fervor for
the Kees enliven its pages, and make it a book as entertaining as it
is enlightening.

Clementine Peterson is respected and admired as an authority on
the Keeshond throughout the world. A breeder of outstanding dogs,
she served as president of the Keeshond Club of America from 1962
to 1968. She has judged the breed from coast to coast (including the
Specialties of the Keeshond Club of America, the Keeshond Club of
Delaware Valley, and the Capital Keeshond Club), and in many for-
eign lands.

Mrs. Peterson, together with her late husband J. Whitney Peterson,
first became interested in the Keeshond in 1941. The Dutch breed,
so alert, fun-loving and gay, beautifully coated and highly intelligent,
found a special place in the family's world of dogs.

Accomplishment has been said to be the result of interest, ability
and talent. To these, Mrs. Peterson added sincerity of purpose
when she accepted my invitation to write the monthly Keeshond
column for *Popular Dogs* in 1953. Today, after 17 years of careful

7

research, analysis and more than 200 columns and featured articles, her writings stand as one of the more important contributions to Keeshond success.

Her knowledgeable columns, even as this book, have always been unbiased and selfless. She has never sought nor expected personal gain for all the time and untiring effort she has put forth in promoting her breed.

We all shared her pleasure as her Keeshond column became more and more popular with readers, regardless of their breeds. Mrs. Peterson includes advice aimed toward the welfare of all breeds as well as the care of the Keeshond. Of great importance, too, was her encouragement of the Keeshond Club of America's "Code of Ethics", reported by her in January 1966. This informative guide for breeders and owners was directed against unplanned, surplus breedings, against unscrupulous advertising, and directed toward the encouragement of the right home for each Keeshond.

The history of "the laughing Dutchman of dogdom", detailing its progress in Europe, England and the United States, is sure to fascinate all readers who love and enjoy dogs.

—Alice Wagner

Preface

THIS book is dedicated to the Keeshond, and to its devoted owners, breeders and exhibitors of the past, present, and future.

I wish to express special tribute to Mrs. Wingfield Digby who was originally responsible for bringing the breed from continental Europe and establishing it in England. We in America, together with Keeshond owners in other countries, owe a great deal to Mrs. Digby and to the many, many others whose British-bred exports have contributed preeminently to the Keeshond's progress in various parts of the world.

Among the early breeders in England, Mrs. Alice Gatacre will always hold a unique place as the author of *The Keeshond,* published in London in 1938. It was the first comprehensive book devoted exclusively to the breed. Although long out of print, it has been an important source of reference on the Keeshond's beginnings in Europe and Britain.

To the Keeshond fanciers everywhere who have stripped their scrapbooks to loan photographs and have cooperated so enthusiastically in every way with my writing of *The Complete Keeshond,* I say "Thank you all!"

Please note that photographs of American-owned Keeshonden have been included only if they have met the following requirements, set by the author, and based on American Kennel Club records:

Dogs having won five or more Groups, or one or more Bests in Show in the United States.

Bitches having won one or more Groups in the United States.

Dogs having sired ten or more American champions.

Bitches having whelped five or more American champions.

Best in Show Braces.

"Famous Firsts", such as the first American champion, national Specialty winner, Obedience titlists, etc.

Winners of Keeshond Club of America Specialties.

Top-ranking Obedience performers.

In addition to everyone cited in the text for their helpfulness in various respects, I greatly appreciate the courtesies extended by *Popular Dogs* magazine; officials and staff members of the American Kennel Club; Mr. Arthur Frederick Jones, former editor of the AKC's *Purebred Dogs—American Kennel Gazette,* and by the *Raad van Beheer op Kynologisch Gebeid in Nederland* (the Kennel Club in Holland) .

—Clementine L. Peterson

In citing the show and producing records of famous Keeshonden, the abbreviations in common usage by the dog fancy have been employed. For the uninitiated, we offer this glossary:

AKC = American Kennel Club

CC = Challenge Certificate

Ch. = Champion

Chs. = Champions
> (In identifying a champion of more than one country, the name of the country is also abbreviated, viz: Am. for American, Eng. for English, Can. for Canadian, etc).

BIS = Best in Show

GR1 = First in Group
> (The word Group is also used alone to indicate a First in Group as in *He won a Group* or *He scored 3 Groups.*)

GR2, GR3, GR4—2nd in Group, 3rd in Group, 4th in Group.
> (The term *Group placements* as used in this book indicates a Group win other than First).

BOB = Best of Breed

BOS = Best of Opposite Sex to the Best of Breed

WD = Winners Dog
> (Winners of each of the male classes compete together for the Winners Dog designation. At American shows, only the Winners Dog—among males—can win points toward his championship.)

WB = Winners Bitch
> (Winners of each of the bitch classes compete together for the Winners Bitch designation. At American shows, only the Winners Bitch—among bitches—can win points toward her championship.)

BOW = Best of Winners
> (The winner between the Winners Dog and Winners Bitch.)

RD = Reserve Winners Dog—runnup to the Winners Dog

RB = Reserve Winners Bitch—runnerup to the Winners Bitch

CD = Companion Dog, Novice Obedience degree

CDX = Companion Dog Excellent, Open Obedience degree

UD = Utility Dog degree

T = Tracking Dog degree

The abbreviation *wh.* with date used in the captions identifies the year in which the dog was whelped.

The Name:

There are a number of theories about the origin of the Dutch name of *Keeshond* for the breed. But first let us clear up any existing confusion concerning definitions of the two syllables in Kees-hond (pronounced *caze-hawnd*).

The word *kees* has no connection with quay or dock, called *kade* and *gracht* in Holland. Nor does it, as many people have jokingly suggested, have anything to do with cheese. Cheese in Dutch is *kaas*. Actually *"Kees"* is a Dutch nickname for Cornelis or Cornelius.

Hond means dog, not hound.

The suffix "en" (as in Keeshonden) is the Dutch plural, and has been adopted here. Frankly, the use of this plural in America seems utterly inappropriate to the author, for it causes no end of grammatical confusion and error in English.

The interesting story that ties the Keeshond's name to that of the Patriot rebellion leader, Cornelis de Gyselaer, is explored in detail in Chapter 3.

13

The Two Navigators, an 1883 portrait of Judge Charles Patrick Daly and his dog, by Edward L. Henry. Sag Harbor, Long Island in background. Courtesy of Mr. and Mrs. John Mayer.

1

The Keeshond—A Family Dog

THE KEESHOND has been known and acclaimed for its qualities as a family companion and watchdog for several centuries in continental Europe, and through recent decades in England, the United States and other parts of the world.

It is natural for dog owners to believe that their own breed is the greatest, but the enthusiasm of Keeshond owners seems to far surpass most of the others. Let us see why.

Wherever the Keeshond is seen, he draws admiring comments from strangers who want to know, "What is that gorgeous dog?" And it is always amusing to be asked if he is gentle, especially when—as is often the case—he is licking the questioner's hand, or her little boy's face.

The American Kennel Club approved Standard describes the Keeshond as a handsome dog of well-balanced, short-coupled body, attracting attention by his alert carriage and intelligent expression, luxurious coat, richly plumed tail well-curled over his back, and by his fox-like face and head with small, pointed ears, mounted high and carried erect. His coat is very thick around the neck, forepart of shoulders and chest, forming a lion-like mane. His rump and hindlegs are also thickly coated down to the hocks, forming the

15

characteristic "trousers". His silver-gray-to-black coloring and markings are added eye-catchers.

Dogs have coats of varying lengths of either smooth, silky, curly, or wiry hair. These coats generally require a considerable amount of grooming at home, or costly professional care, to keep them from matting or to provide fashionable trimming or plucking. Many also have a "doggy" odor which requires frequent bathing. The smooth-coated dogs are often sensitive to hot, cold and wet weather.

But the Keeshond is a hardy dog, needs no trimming, and the texture of his coat is quite different from that of other breeds. It is actually *fur,* an attribute mainly found in breeds of northern origin. This type of coat consists of straight, harsh guard hairs, standing well out from a thick, downy undercoat. It is *odorless,* sheds water, seldom mats, is easily taken care of (as explained in the chapter on General Care), and its density helps keep out insects. The coat also contributes to the breed's adaptability to various climates, and is often compared to the Arabs' woolen burnoose, worn alike as insulation against the desert's blazing heat or nighttime cold. Incidentally, Keeshond fur is hand-spun into knitting yarn in England and the United States.

The officially approved coat color is a mixture of shadings of gray to black. In each dog the coloration should range from palest gray or cream (almost white) in the undercoat and on the legs, trousers, and tail plume, to black on the tips of the guard hairs. But it is impossible to adequately depict in words, or even photographs, the subtlety of the shadings which produce the distinctive markings of the breed.

To the casual observer, all Keeshonden may seem to look alike, and even people who should know better have been known to say just that. But it is not the case. In fact, notwithstanding the many Best in Show wins by different Kees braces throughout the country, it is difficult to match up two of the breed for a brace. One reason is that the overall effect of the coloring in individual dogs may legitimately vary from light to very dark. The degree of the variation is mainly governed by the length and quantity of the black tips on the guard hairs, and the location and density of these hairs on the different parts of the dog. However, it should be noted that under the Standard, "any pronounced deviation from the gray color is not permissible."

16

The Standard states "the ideal height of fully matured dogs (over two years old), measured from top of withers to the ground, is: for males, 18 inches; bitches, 17 inches. Length of back from withers to rump should equal height."

In other words, the Keeshond is a compact, medium-sized dog, whose shoulder height under his fur is approximately an inch below the seat of the average straight chair. His size, coupled with his robust build, ready-for-anything nature and other characteristics, make him an all-round dog, appealing to both men and women, and particularly acceptable to modern living in either small or large homes.

Appearance and size are, of course, important considerations in acquiring a dog. But temperament is far more important. After all, the most beautiful dog in the world can be an utter failure as a pet, a show dog, or an obedience worker if he doesn't have the right temperament, and the ability to learn what is required of him. This focuses attention on the fact that the general traits of character found in different breeds are chiefly the inherited results of the specific purposes for which the breed has been developed in the past.

As one of the most affectionate and lovable of all dogs, the Keeshond has the distinction of having been bred for centuries for its qualities as a family companion and sensible watchdog. It is not inclined to roam as are many of the hunting breeds, nor has it been developed to kill other animals or to be an attack dog. These factors have undoubtedly contributed to its contentment as a home-loving, gentle pet, and to the special fondness for children for which the Keeshond is renowned. It is also fortunate that through selective breeding, breeders in the United States and other countries have continued to put special emphasis on maintaining this breed's typical, excellent temperament.

Kees give their devotion to everyone in the family and are seldom "one man" dogs. This explains their ability, at any age, to happily adapt themselves to new homes. All they seem to need, or want, is to be loved and to please their owners.

Although wary of strangers and keenly alert as alarm-giving watchdogs, Kees are not attackers or "yappers." They quickly turn off the "alarm" and with paw extended, offer their friendship to people who are admitted to the home.

17

Another typical trait is amiability with other dogs. In fact, the breed has become well-known on this score in the dog show world because of the unusual benching arrangements it makes possible. As an example, for three years the Keeshond benches were show-stoppers at the Eastern Dog Club's two-day show in Boston where Mrs. Virginia Cowley, owner of Nether-Lair Kennels, benched 30 to 40 Kees *without any partitions* between them. All but a few of the dogs had never seen each other before or been to a show. Despite this, the dogs quietly spent two long days in those strange surroundings. They snoozed or played with their bench-mates, and with wagging tails and happy faces, seemed to revel in the petting and admiration of the crowds which gathered around them. With the same results, unpartitioned benching has been used for from 20 to 65 Kees at other shows such as the Specialties of the Keeshond Club of Southern California, the Capital Keeshond Club in Washington, D.C., the Nor-Cal Club's entries at Golden Gate in San Francisco, and by many individual exhibitors of four or more entries. I wonder how many other breeds could be benched this way?

The Keeshond's instinctively clean personal habits are both amusing and practical. From the time they can totter to their feet, most Kees puppies will stagger to a newspaper in the middle of the floor to use it as intended. Grown dogs try to remove burrs and such from their own and their housemates' fur with their teeth, and they lick paws and wash their faces like cats. Owners who take their Kees on boats find they automatically go to the lee side to lift a leg by the railing, and will leave their droppings in a sandbox placed on deck for the purpose. The reasons for these traits of cleanliness can be quite baffling until we consider the possible effects of the centuries during which the breed lived in the confined quarters of water-craft and farm houses, where the meticulous Dutch and other European housewives would not tolerate "dirty dogs".

It is easy to train the Keeshond for almost any purpose because he is so gentle and eager to please his owners. To him, it appears to be a catastrophe to be scolded or even scowled at, and his response to praise is ecstatic. Harsh words or treatment are therefore unnecessary and should never be used. In addition, the high level of his intelligence makes him quick to learn and sure to remember what he has been taught. No wonder the breed has a reputation as a "natural" in Obedience, and has chalked up outstanding individual and team performance records in Trials.

The bench show achievements by Keeshonden are most impressive, and show that this breed, although comparatively small in the number of annual registrations, is high in show quality and temperament. What's more, contrary to the general belief that all successful show dogs live a life apart from their owners, almost all of the top-winning Kees are house-pets, and are owner-trained and handled.

The happy, affectionate, and adaptable nature of the Keeshond, his intelligence and desire to learn whatever is required of him, combined with his many other qualities, make him an all-round companion for people of all ages and interests. And his great beauty is an added source of pleasure and pride for his owners. Just ask anyone who has a Keeshond in the family.

U.S. Supreme Court Justice William O. Douglas being greeted by Mrs. Alfred McCormack's Ch. Keeshaven's Clown and his owner-breeder at a 1958 Washington D.C. reception. Story, page 97.

2

Development
of the Keeshond's Character

WHAT has made the Keeshond the treasured family companion,
the prized obedience performer, and the show dog of distinction
that he is in the United States and other countries today? For some
of the answer, we look to the breed's origins, its natural instincts
and its development—a fascinating story that began far back in the
past.

The inherent, general characteristics of the Keeshond—and of
every other breed—have not been developed in just a few years. Or
even a few decades. They have evolved through countless centuries,
as results of the ways in which Man has used the dog to serve his
needs and desires.

Since prehistoric time, Man has employed the help of the dog
in many ways—for hunting game, herding and guarding flocks,
protecting homes from animal and human marauders, for killing
rodents, for rescue work or for use as draft animals. The specific
purpose for which the various breeds were used, their training,
their environment—all have joined forces with the natural laws of
heredity to mold the temperaments, physical structures, and other

attributes of the breeds into the patterns in which they now exist.

Modern methods of meat production, travel, control of animal pests, and other advancements of civilization have, with few exceptions, put such uses of the dog into the category of sport or hobby, rather than of need. As a result, the most important role of almost every breed today is that of an all-round family dog.

It is now very important that the dog's temperament and other characteristics fit him for present-day living in the home. However, to a great extent, this will have been shaped by the breed's historical background, and the part that the home environment has played in it. In other words, for how many generations, and to what degree, has it been a breed that has had close association with owners and their families, and how much of this has been in the homes?

The Keeshond in America has been recognized as exceptional in many ways, both by the public and by qualified authorities on dogs. It is significant that he is often referred to as "the laughing Dutchman", "the gentleman from Holland", a canine gentleman", and is registered by the American Kennel Club as one of the Non-Sporting breeds—the companion dogs.

This recognition of his typical temperament, and the breed's official classification, did not come about by chance. As the interesting and unique story of the Keeshond unfolds, we will see that this is one of the few breeds which throughout its history has *not* been bred to hunt, kill animals, or chase and attack criminals. For several centuries, it has been raised just for its qualities as a family companion, and as a sensible, alarm-giving watchdog. So let's turn back the clock for a short glimpse into this interesting history.

3

Early History of the Keeshond

THE story of the Keeshond, as it comes to us down through the ages, is fascinating and filled with contrasts. He is an ancient breed, well-known in some parts of the world, a newcomer in others, and completely unheard of in still others. He has been a dog of the people, and a dog of the nobility. His popularity made him famous as the national emblem of an 18th century rebellious political party in Holland, and in turn, caused his relegation to semi-obscurity.

But since time immemorial, he apparently has had much the same general appearance, and the same inherent characteristics that make him a loyal companion and watchdog for mankind. If the breed had a coat of arms, its Latin heraldic inscription might well be *"Immutatus et Fidelis"*, Unchanged and Faithful.

Through the recorded findings of paleontologists from many countries over the last three centuries, the Keeshond has gradually emerged from the mists surrounding his prehistoric ancestry. The 18th and 19th century works of such eminent authorities as Ludwig Rutimeyer in Switzerland, Brinkman in Scandinavia, Count

23

Poutiatin in Russia, and Linne in France, together with the more recent findings of Gandert (France, 1930), H. Santo (Japan, 1957), and Erich Schneider-Leyer (Germany, 1964) have traced the Keeshond back to fossil remains of *Canis Familiaris Palustris* of the *Neolithic* or Late Stone Age (5000 B.C.), found mainly in northern areas of the globe.

This brings us a mental picture of cave dwellers huddled around a fire, with a furry-coated, wolf-like dog curled up at the entrance as guardian—much the same picture that we have of the Keeshond and his function today, but with a few improvements in the modern family's cave.

There is general agreement on the generic classification of the Keeshond as a *Spitz* breed. In 1867, Fitzinger listed 48 different varieties of Spitz. Among the large number researched and pictured in Dr. Schneider-Leyer's 1964 *Dogs of the World* we find the Swedish *Vastogaspets* (which look like Corgis), a Russian *Laika,* Norwegian *Buhund,* Lapland *Spitz* and the Swedish *Grahund.* Better known modern Spitz are the Samoyed, Siberian Husky, Alaskan Malamute, Esquimaux Dog, Chow Chow, Japanese Akita, Finnish Spitz, Norwegian Elkhound, German Wolfsspitz, Dutch Keeshond, and Pomeranian. The kinship of these and other Spitz breeds can be seen at a glance from their similarity in structure, coat composition, foxy heads, prick ears, and (excepting the Schipperke) tails carried over the back.

The Samoyed is widely credited on canine geneaological charts with being the "top man on the totem pole"—the first historically known progenitor of Spitz dogs, and the direct ancestor of the Keeshond. Dr. Schneider-Leyer says of the Samoyed that since ancient time "this large dog with the smiling face" has served primitive, nomadic Samoyed tribes as sled dog, reindeer-herder, and guardian of his master's property in northwest Asia and northern Europe, and has lived in close fellowship with man. In regard to color, the book relates that after the Samoyed's comparatively recent introduction to North America and Alaska, breeders favored the white and cream forms over the breed's previously gray, brown or black coloration.

But how did the Keeshond fit into this genealogic, geographic and historical jig-saw puzzle? How, when, and where did the breed become known in Europe?

24

Greek wine jug,
circa 400 B.C.

18th century crystal goblet
depicting the Keeshond as
the symbol of the Dutch
Patriot Party's revolt against
the reigning House of
Orange. *Boymans Museum,*
Rotterdam.

The Dog of New South Wales & the Pomeranian Dog. Engraving, London, 1803.
Courtesy of Mrs. Frank Taussig.

Europe

It is generally supposed that the ancestor of the Dutch Keeshond and his German counterpart originally came from the north on ancient water craft. When and where this first occurred is subject to conjecture, based on scattered bits and pieces of evidence and legends.

The design on an Athenian wine jug of about 400 B.C. depicts a Keeshond-like dog (page 25). Portrayals of similar dogs on other antique objects ranging from tombstones to gold coins have been unearthed in different countries and have understandably been claimed as substantiation of the antiquity of the Keeshond and the Pomeranian. The theory accepted by some authorities that the Pom evolved as a small version of Spitz breeds in Germany, where it was called *Zuerg Spitz* (Dwarf Spitz), seems plausible from the context and illustrations in among other works, Vero Shaw's *Book of the Dog* (1881) and G M. Hicks' *The Pomeranian* (1906).

Alice Gatacre's classic book, *The Keeshond* (1938), cites a Spanish legend mentioned in *Dog and Man* by Sloan and Farquar, telling about three dogs called *Cubillon, Melampo* and *Lubino* who accompanied their masters to Bethlehem to worship the Christ child. The word "Lubino" could have been Lu*p*ino, *b* and *p* being interchangeable in Latin languages. *Lupo* means *wolf* in modern Italian, and the Keeshond has been called *Lupino* and *Volpino* in Italy. The French name for the breed is *Chien Loup* (Wolf Dog) and *Grand Lou Lou*.

Amsterdam and the Keeshond

The crude life and times of early inhabitants of the man-made mud-flats of Friesland, where Vikings raided the northern shores of what is now the Netherlands, are a far cry from a 1959 party by a swimming pool in Redding, Connecticut. But at that party, the author met George Masselman, a noted Dutch historian and writer. He related the legend and history of the founding of Amsterdam, in which ancestors of the Keeshond played a prominent role. At my request, Mr. Masselman kindly sent me details of his fascinating narrative for publication in *Popular Dogs* magazine.

27

The story began in Friesland eons ago. Chronicles tell us that the Friesians developed laws to keep peace among themselves. One law had to do with dogs: "He who kills a hunting dog shall be fined 8 pieces, but if he kills someone's pet dog the fine shall be 12 pieces." This may well be one of the earliest indications of where the dog had become more important to man as a friend than as a hunter.

The period from about 800 to 1000 A D. was a grim one for the Friesians. Vikings killed, enslaved and plundered them in hit-and-run attacks on the shores of western Europe. It was in this period that the legend and historical founding of Amsterdam had their beginnings.

A Viking ship is said to have foundered on the Friesland coast near Stavoren, and all hands were drowned except one—a chieftain's son. Accompanied by his dog, a Friesian fisherman named Wolfert, who was a Christian, rescued the invader, and the two men and the dog set sail on Wolfert's fishing boat. In the dead of night a fierce storm drove them south, deep into unknown waters, but they finally drifted to safety onto high ground. In gratitude for their deliverance, Wolfert and the Norseman built a small chapel, which they dedicated to St. Olaf, patron saint of mariners. Wolfert's dog was witness to all this. Here the legend ends, and straight history takes over.

In the course of time, a small fishing village came into being on the spot where Wolfert's boat is supposed to have landed—the spot where the Amstel river flowed into the inland sea. A series of great storms during the 13th century widened and deepened nearby waters until it became the Zuider Zee. A dam was built across the river, and the little town came to be known as *Amstelredam*. No one could have guessed it would become the metropolis of Amsterdam.

The people of Amsterdam never forgot the legend or the dog. To carry a dog on a vessel was first considered a good omen, and developed into a custom. In time the dog became part of the sea laws because it came to represent ownership. No one dared ransack a ship if a dog was on board.

The Great Seal of Amsterdam shows an ancient vessel with a dog on its deck. What breed was this dog? When we look at its face peering over the gunnels of the ship on the Seal, there can be little doubt.

The Great Seal of *Amstelredam* (Amsterdam), Holland. Courtesy of Yale
University Library, New Haven, Conn.

29

Pomeranians. Illustration from Vero Shaw's *Illustrated Book of the Dog*. London, 1881.

The author is grateful to Mr. Masselman for the glimpses he has given us into the Keeshond's distant past, and to Christopher Becker, a professor of history and Keeshond Club of America member, who located (in the Yale library at New Haven, Connecticut) the replica of the Seal pictured in this book.

Germany

Man-made boundaries of countries are not barriers to the migration of dogs, nor do they necessarily determine a breed's name or nationality. Whether the Nordic Spitz-dog ancestors of the Keeshond first arrived in parts of Europe now known as The Netherlands, or in Germany, or wherever else, and when this actually took place, is still debatable and may always be. The preponderance of evidence gives credence to the theory that the dog called the Keeshond in Holland and the one called Wolfsspitz in Germany were the same breed. It may have come directly to ancient Friesland from the North, or on barges from the Schwartzwald (Black Forest) and Wurttemberg, or crossed the frontiers from Westphalia and the Rhineland into the Netherlands. At any rate, we now turn to the 15th century in Germany.

The German scholar Bachman believes that the first known mention of the name *Spitz* was made in an edict by Count Eberhard zu Sayne, a feudal land holder in the Rhine Valley in 1450, forbidding his retainers use of the word *Spitzhund* as an invective. Dr. Caius, founder of Caius College, Cambridge, referred to the Germanic Pomeranian dog in his 1570 treatise, *De Cannibus Brittanicus*. Also at about that time, the German version of *Reynard the Fox* described as a Spitz dog the character in that story who was the defender of the homestead.

Some authorities say that the Schnauzer, a breed dating from the 15th century, was orginated by crossing the black German *Pudel* (Poodle) with the Wolfsspitz and wirehaired Pinscher, an indication that the Keeshond's somewhat larger counterpart, the gray-shaded Wolfsspitz, was known in Germany in very early times.

Evidence from many sources shows that over a long period, several varieties of Spitz evolved in Germany, ranging in size and coloration from the *Great White Spitz* and *Grosse Grau Wolfsspitz* (large, gray, wolf-colored) to the smaller *Pommer* (Pomeranian

31

White Keeshond in 18th century cut. Meissen porcelain figurine, Germany, circa 1820. From the Lord Northcliffe Meissen collection in England. Photo courtesy of Mrs. T. Bedford Davie.

Keeshond in trim fashionable in Europe, 18th century. Dutch tile plaque, circa 1790. Courtesy, Shelburne Museum, Shelburne, Vt.

Life-sized, glazed terra-cotta statue. Italy, circa 1830. Owned by the author.

Typical Wolfsspitz, Aus. &
Germ. Ch. Max I, wh. 1896.

Typical short-backed Wurt-
temberger House-Spitz, Ch.
Mentor Holsatia, wh. 1899.

Int. Ch. Lux, wh. 1893.

dog). In the late 17th and early 18th centuries, a largish White Spitz was raised in Pomerania and other provinces, and black and brown varieties in Wurttemberg and elsewhere, and were used to guard vineyards, farmhouses, and boats. The breed is depicted in monuments in Stuttgart and Bochum, one a memorial to the Vinegrowers of the Rhineland, and the other commemorating the Herdsmen. In addition, the small Spitz—about 11 to 12 inches high and with the same coat color as his bigger relatives—became a popular house dog.

In 1899, German breeders formed the *Verein fur Deutsche Spitz* (German Spitz Club), a national organization which issued Standards and established a Stud Book and rules governing registration. Since then, matters having to do with the German Spitz breeds have been under the jurisdiction of the German Spitz Club in much the same way that the American Kennel Club officiates for all breeds here.

The first German Spitz Stud Book was published in 1913. The total number of large and small Spitz listed was 1,050, most of which had been whelped from 1891 to 1898. Of the 699 large varieties, 247 were white, 222 were black, 221 wolf-gray, 1 orange, 7 red, and 1 parti-colored.

In the author's opinion, the time has come for us in the United States to *do* something other than wring our hands about the unscrupulous breeding and commercialization of purebred dogs which has grown rampant in America. The German Spitz Club has done something about the problem in Germany. I therefore strongly believe that the Club's following rules, translated and sent to me in 1960 by Mr. Becker, warrant serious consideration for possible adaptation and adoption in America:

> Litters and older dogs are not registrable in the German Spitz Club Stud Book unless both parents have been awarded one of the three standard show certifications: *Gut* (Good), *Sehr Gut* (Very Good), or *Vorzuglich* (Excellent). Nor can dogs of any age be registered if they have previously passed through the hands of unreliable persons.
>
> Anyone who is an amateur or professional handler may become a member, but the Club's rules specify that: "Commercial dog dealers and persons probably engaged in the buying and selling of dogs bred by others, in mercenary and irresponsible fashion, and exhibitors belonging to associations of dog dealers or taking part in their activities, may not become members." Further, in 1958, the Spitz Club

Eng. Ch. Ado von Thierlstein, imported from Germany by Mrs. Alice Gatacre. *Photo by Fall.*

denied the use of the Stud Book to persons selling dogs to dealers, and expressed these reasons: "Unfortunately there are still a few breeders who breed without planning, care little for type and soundness, and therefore, seldom exhibit their dogs at shows and sell some of their inferior puppies to dog dealers. It ought to be perfectly evident that such actions have a very bad effect on the breed."

Holland

We now return, in time and place, to the misty shores of Holland, the land where the Keeshond became nationally and internationally famous.

After the founding of Amstelredam in the late 13th century, and the significant inclusion of the Dutch dog portrayed on the Great Seal of Amsterdam, we hear of the dog only vaguely over the next several centuries. However, subsequent history shows that during this dim period, the breed became widely known in continental Europe.

Since early times, most barges, farms and carts had a canine sentry, usually a Keeshond or whatever name he was given in the various countries. He was also a guard for flocks and sometimes used to hunt skunks. But we must dispel the notion, often expressed even today, that the dog ever *pulled* barges. As an 18-inch high animal, how could he? Barges were cargo vessels with living quarters for the Captain and his family, and the dogs lived on board as zealous guardians of their owners' properties and playmates for their children.

Kees and *Spitz* are defined in very early Dutch and German dictionaries as "rabble", a possible indication of the prevalence of the breed in both countries. Oostoeck's *Illustrated Encyclopedia* describes the Keeshond as "also called Spitz hond. A watch dog with a fairly long, bushy coat, especially round the neck, with long hairs forming a ruff; most commonly seen in white, but also existing in black and in gray. The latter variety is called '*Brabantsche Keezen*'. The Dwarf Keeshond or Toy Pomeranian is kept as a lady's pet."

Historical events in the Netherlands in the late 1700s, combined with the breed's popularity in that country, made the Keeshond internationally known in Europe. In about 1781, Holland was divided into two political factions: the *Orangists* (conservatives) who supported the Prince of Orange as governor of the Netherlands, and the rebellious *Patriots* (or *Keezen,* as the pro-Orange men derisively referred to the people's party members.) Cornelis de Gyselaar, who had one of these popular dogs as his constant companion, was a leader in the Patriots' revolt. Remembering that "Kees" is a nickname in the Netherlands for Cornelis or Cornelius (see page 13), it seems significant in regard to a basis for the breed's name that "Kees" de Gyselaar's "hond" became the emblem of the Dutch party.

It was fashionable in those days to trim the Keeshond in a Poodle type cut, the comical results of which can be seen in the pictures of Keeshonden on political pamphelts and other objects of the period reproduced on page 39. The 18th century Dutch tile plaque depicting a Keeshond in the same trim, hangs in the kitchen of the Vermont House in Shelburne Museum, Shelburne, Vermont, where the author first saw it during a New England dog show circuit.

The fact that the Keeshond was the 18th century Patriot Party's symbol and the Pug represented the Orangists is comparable to the roles played by the donkey and elephant in United States' politics today, and may be the basis for the erroneous reference to the Keeshond as "the national dog of Holland". Officials in the Netherlands Consulate in New York City have assured the author that to their knowledge, Holland has never had a "national" dog.

It is believed that after suppression of the Patriots' rebellion, many Kees were done away with for fear that possession of the dogs would indicate affiliation with the defeated rebels. Thus this beautiful and popular breed paradoxically became the victim of its own fame. Although some barge captains and farmers retained their dogs, and kept informal stud records for their own use, it was more than a century later before the Keeshond again came to public attention.

According to Mrs. Gatacre, Miss J. G. Van der Blom, who was actively connected with the breed in Holland, Germany and England, and—much later—Baroness van Hardenbroek van de Kleine Lindt, are largely credited with revival of Kees in Holland. Miss van der Blom showed her first Keeshond in 1891 in Amsterdam. Five Kees were entered, three grays and two whites, one of the whites being of German origin.

As one of many subsequent examples of the countries, colors and

Dutch political lampoons of the 18th century depicting the Keeshond, emblem of the Patriots, in the popular trim of the time. From the *Prenten Kabinet*, Amsterdam.

Engraving of painting by George Stubbs (1724–1803), England. Courtesy of Mrs. Frank Taussig.

Miss J. G. van der Blom's German Wolfsspitz, shown in Holland about 1915.

sizes involved, two other Dutch breeders in 1901 imported to Holland white *Overweight Pomeranians* (as they were then called in England), and brought in from Germany black descendants of a famous German black dog, Othello. Mrs. Gatacres tells us "Othello was rumoured to be a giant, too big for a typical black Keeshond, whilst the white English Overweight Poms were often considered too small and were centered at shows as 'Dwerg' Keeshonden."

In 1907, Keeshonden were divided into English and German-Dutch types in Dutch shows. The next year, a Standard of Points, published in a dog magazine—*De Nederlandsche Hondensport,* prescribed size as "Whites and Blacks to measure at least 16 inches at the shoulder, Grays at least 18 inches, weight 40 pounds." The present American Standard (see page 141) closely follows the Dutch, British and German standards except for size in the German Gray variety, which calls for "at least 18 inches at the shoulder, *the larger the better."* The italics are the author's.

In 1910, Miss van der Blom imported among others, the gray German Ch. Fritz vom Harz, and along with other Hollanders, produced many winners through breeding German dogs to native Dutch Keeshonden. As the number of breeders increased, Miss Van der Blom tried to start a branch of the German *Verein fur Deutsche Spitz* in Holland, but Dutch fanciers preferred independence. The *Nederlandse Keeshond Club* was established in 1924, and has been a vital force in the breed. (In 1967, Herr Huig van Wingerden, the club's president for the five years preceding his 1967 vice-presidency, came to America where he judged 128 Kees in the Keeshond Club of Delaware Valley's Specialty show in Devon, Pa.)

During World War I, the breed in Germany suffered for lack of available food and was greatly reduced in numbers. To improve his stock, Herr Saloman, the only large scale breeder of German Wolfsspitz, sent a bitch to be bred to Miss Van der Blom's Ch. Teddy. From the litter, two came to Holland, Baroness van Hardenbroek's Fredl am Ziel and Baron Scheidius's Faust am Ziel.

Starting around 1925, the Baroness' successful breeding and showing of her van Walhalla Kennel Kees did a great deal to make the Keeshond better known in Holland and other countries. She bought one of her early dogs, her famous Ch. Bart, from gypsies in a caravan. Bart's pedigree was short and typical of the Dutch-bred Kees of the time: "Sired by Fik, ancestors unknown, ex Pol, sire and dam, Fix

41

and Fikske." But Bart's picture (page 43) indicates he could do well in American rings today.

Baroness van Hardenbroek was also an early leader of Dutch opposition to the persistent German efforts to have the Keeshond in Holland officially named *German Spitz*. As late as 1960 a similar attempt to change the breed's name was made through the *Federation Cynologique Internationale* (International Dog Federation), arbiter of purebred dog matters in continental Europe. But further resistance by Dutch Keeshond fanciers evidently won the long battle on the subject.

In response to the author's 1969 letter of inquiry as to the breed's official name in the Netherlands, the *Raad van Beheer op Kynologisch Gebied in Nederland* (Dutch Kennel Club) replied, "The Keeshond is registered in our country as *Keeshond*. According to the international standard of the breed published by the Federation Internationale, the following colours are approved for registration and exhibition: grey, black, white and brown." And added, "In 1968 a total of 81 Keeshonds were registered in our stud book: 76 grey and 5 white."

Over the years, many other Dutch breeders contributed much to the breed's progress. Notable among them was Mrs. Alice Gatacre, who raised the gray, white and black forms in her native province of Guelderland. After her marriage, Mrs. Gatacre became a resident of England, and Holland's loss was Britain's and the English-speaking world's gain, as will be seen in the chapter on Kees in England.

Sparked by the desire to learn about Keeshonden in Holland, and the expectation that we would find Kees and people who knew about them wherever we went, Mr. Peterson and the author set sail on the Dutch liner S/S Nieuw Amsterdam in 1954. On the ship we had our first surprise: the word Keeshond meant nothing to all but one of the Dutch passengers and staff. The exception was the ship's Captain, who vaguely recalled that the dogs had been widely used in the past as guards on water-craft. We found much the same reactions in Holland itself. And during motor trips throughout the country, saw no Keeshonden on canal boats or in the towns, and only two near farms.

Fortunately, correspondence with the Dutch Kennel Club had provided a list of breeders. In the homes and kennels visited, it was a pleasure to find so many lovely Kees, great enthusiasm about the breed and such gracious hospitality.

In some instances, the breeders—in line with their carefully

Baroness van Hardenbroek's Hans, Ada and Anke van Walhalla, Dutch winners circa 1935.

Dutch Ch. Bart. Owner, Baroness van Hardenbroek van der Kleine Lindt.

Mrs. Bloemen-Russel's de Klep Kooi Keeshonden, Helvoirt, Holland, 1954.

Chilean Ch. Marco v.d. Krashof taking Best in Show, Vina del Mar, Chile, 1952. Breeder: Van den Krashof Kennels, Holland.

South African Chs. Sigelinski's Marjan and Siem.
Breeder: Sigelinski Kennels, Holland. Ch. Siem,
Best in Show, South Africa, 1960. Owner: Mrs. E.
Ficker, Johannesburg.

planned breeding programs—had imported English studs to increase size. The uniformity of good quality in the dogs was impressive. But the ones we wanted to bring home were not for sale. Regretfully, we left that delightful country empty-handed.

Two years before going to Holland, the author had a startling experience in South America. By chance, I went to an all-breed show in Vina del Mar, Chile. At the exact moment I arrived, the crowds around the Best-in-Show ring were clapping wildly and shouting "Bravo!" "Ole!" for the winner. It was a Keeshond. I thought I was dreaming. But my conversation with the dog's owners, a charming Britisher and her Dutch husband, revealed that they had imported the BIS winner, Ch. Marco van den Krashof, from Holland the month before. His win in Vina del Mar was his second BIS in Chile, and his quality indicated that he could be outstanding in any country's show rings.

The Keeshond's historical role in 18th century Holland inspired the name, and the activities of English breeders in the 20th century provided the impetus which led to the breed's being known and exhibited in its gray-to-black shaded form as the *Dutch Keeshond* in many parts of the world including Africa, Australia, Bermuda, Canada, Chile, Cuba, Mexico, New Zealand, Rhodesia and the Scandinavian countries.

Mrs. Wingfield Digby in 1962, with gifts and honors received from admirers around the world in tribute to her 60 years of devotion to Keeshonden.

4

The Keeshond in England

THE British have long been world famous for their successful breeding of many breeds, due to their ability and willingness to devote the time, effort and knowledge necessary to produce and export good dogs. The high quality of the English-bred Keeshonds sent to America ever since 1930 are cases in point. In fact, with few exceptions, the breed in our country has been based on British-bred Kees, which stem from originally combining Dutch and German Kees in England. Consequently, the breed's background in England, and the British breeders whose exports have had an outstanding impact on the development of the Keeshond in America, are featured in this chapter.

We have learned from the findings of paleontologists that the Keeshond is generically a variety of Spitz. We also know from the works of many authoritative British writers of the 1800's and Mrs. Gatacre's book, *The Keeshond* (1938), that Spitz of various colors—white, cream, grayish-beige, wolf-gray and parti-colored—were first known in England under such names as *Fox Dog, Pomeranian Dog, Wolf Dog* and Overweight Pomeranian.

Graphic evidence in the form of paintings by famous 18th century artists further show that this dog, by whatever name, was a fashionable pet of the nobility and other prominent personages in the

British Isles as far back as during the last four decades of the 1700s. Mrs. Gatacre wrote that:

> The breed seems to have been popular with the Hanoverian kings. Not only did the court of George III possess a Spitz, but I am told that George IV's favorite dog was a Wolfsspitz. A painting of this dog now hangs in Slane Castle, county Meath, and Baroness Burton tells me the dog is an exact replica of her Keeshond, Dochfour Hendrik, 'only rather shorter on the leg'.

Members of the species are depicted in many family portraits by such renowned painters as Thomas Gainsborough, Johann Zoffany, George Stubbs, Sir Joshua Reynolds, W. R. Bigg and others. The paintings are to be found in museums and private art collections in England and the United States, and attest to the high regard that the owners of these dogs had for their pets.

Among the large number of art works mentioned in *The Keeshond,* the best known are Gainsborough's *George III and His Court, The Morning Walk,* and *Mrs. Robinson as "Perdita";* Zoffany's *The William Young Family* and *Music Party on the Thames;* Sir Joshua Reynolds' *William Brummell and his brother George Bryan* (afterward known as *Beau Brummell),* and W. R. Bigg's *Dulce Donum,* or *The Return From School.*

The dogs portrayed were either white, cream or grayish-beige. A few were wolf-sable. In *The Prince of Wales Phaeton* by Stubbs (1724–1803), which hangs in Windsor Castle, the dog was a black-and-white parti-color. A large colored print of the Stubbs painting was acquired by the author, thanks to Mrs. James MacMartin, a founder of the Capital Keeshond Club, who ran across it in an old print shop in Maryland. (See page 49).

Note of interest for California fanciers: The 1949 American edition of Oliver Millar's book, *Thomas Gainsborough,* includes a portrait of Karl Friedrich Abel with a white Spitz curled up at his feet, the original of which is in the Henry E. Huntington Library and Art Gallery in San Marino, California.

Gainsborough is known to have been commissioned to do portraits of dogs alone. It was therefore exceedingly interesting to the author to see recently, in a private home in Connecticut, a Gainsborough of a white Spitz circa 1774 entitled *Lady Ann Fitzpatrick's Fox Dog.* The beautiful painting was in the collection of the Earl of Upper

Above, *The Prince of Wales Phaeton.* Original in Windsor Castle, England, by George Stubbs (1724–1803). Print owned by the author.

Right, *Lady Ann Fitzpatrick's Fox Dog* by Thomas Gainsborough, circa 1774. From the collection of the Earl of Upper Ossory, Ireland. Courtesy of a Fitzpatrick family descendant in Connecticut.

Ossory in Ireland before it came into the possession of its present owner, who is a descendant of the Fitzpatrick family.

The Sportsman's Cabinet, in 1803, described the Pomeranian dog as:

> . . . but little more than 18 or 20 inches in height, distinguished by his long, thick and rather upright coat, forming a tremendous ruff around the neck. The coloration, mostly cream, some white, black, and occasionally parti-colored. With a large bushy tail, curled in a ring on the back. The breed is common to Holland.

William Youatt, in his book *"The Dog,"* in 1845, wrote that the Wolf Dog was no longer needed in Great Britain to protect sheep as formerly, "but he is useful for that purpose in various parts of the Continent." In 1833 a pair of Wolf Dogs were brought to the London Zoological Society where "they were an ornament to the Gardens for a long time. They were mostly covered by white or gray, or occasionally black hair." And "the dogs appeared to have considerable strength, but to be too gentle to contend with a wolf."

The year after the English Kennel Club recognized the Pomeranian in 1870, three Overweight white specimens appeared in the rings; the average weight of the variety at that time was 12 to 20 pounds. Years later, Queen Victoria's fondness for Poms led to her raising them at Windsor Castle, and is credited with making the breed fashionable in the 1890s (page 51).

When we note the size and general appearance of the "Pomeranians" in the engraving by a German artist reproduced here from Vero Shaw's 1881 *Book of the Dog,* the similarity to the Keeshond is arresting, to say the least. The relationship of the Pomeranian to the Keeshond is also brought out in C. M. Hicks' book, *The Pomeranian* (England, 1906), which states that the first "shaded sable Pomeranian" was shown in London in 1899 (page 55). The dog had been sent as a Keeshond to a Miss Beverly in Britain by friends in Holland, but "Kees" as she called him, caused much discussion in British dog publications as to the correct breed name for him. Among the authorities quoted by Hicks, the consensus appears to have been that "Miss Beverly's 'Kees'" could be classified as a "Pomeranian Dog, Keeshond, Wolfsspitz or Spitz". And the furor subsided. Although "Kees" was never bred, there is evidence that a number of sable-shaded Overweight Poms were bred in England around the turn of the 20th century.

50

Price, with 4 pages extra, Twopence.

The British Fancier

OR
KENNEL, POULTRY, PIGEON & PET-STOCK REVIEW

No. 1. Vol. I.   FRIDAY, JANUARY 29, 1892.   { Registered at the General Post Office as a } { Newspaper, and for Transmission abroad }   Price, 2d. ; POST FREE 2½d.

DIEU ET MON DROIT

The Queens Favourite

Dog Windsor Marco

Queen Victoria's Windsor Marco.

The British *Kennel Club* withdrew Challenge Certificates for Overweight Pomeranians in 1916, and the variety was not officially heard from again until it was accepted for registration in 1925 under the name of *Dutch Barge Dogs*. Meanwhile, a tour of Holland by a young English girl had laid the foundation for great and lasting enthusiasm for Keeshonds in Great Britain.

As the founder of the breed in England, with a lifelong dedication to Keeshonds, Mrs. Wingfield Digby, owner of the famous Van Zaandam Kennel, can well be named "The British First Lady of Keesdom". While yachting in Holland with her parents in 1905, Mrs. Digby (then Miss Hamilton-Fletcher) found the beautiful watchdogs seen on Dutch barges so appealing that she bought two wolf-gray puppies from a gold-earringed skipper. Those original "Van Zaandams" were christened Barkles and Zaandam, and were followed to England by Schie, Edam, Dirk, and Cornelius. Later, Lieut. Colonel and Mrs. Wingfield Digby also obtained a number of dogs from Germany for their kennel at Sherborne Castle in Dorset. Others in the British Isles became interested in Keeshonds and brought over more imports from Holland and Germany.

Though the Dutch-bred imports bred true, their pedigrees were often merely informal stud records kept by the barge captains and others who raised these dogs for watchdogs on boats and farms. On the other hand, most of the German-bred members of the breed were officially registered, a situation which may somewhat account for the number of German Wolfsspitz brought to England in the early 1900s.

The first Dutch Barge Dogs were shown in 1923. They were Mrs. Digby's Breda and Saanie and drew much favorable comment in the British press.

The breed was officially renamed Keeshond in 1926, with a Standard much the same as it is today in England and the United States. In 1928, the Kennel Club allotted Challenge Certificates for Keeshonds, and that year seven received CC's.

To explain all the complexities of British dog show procedure, and the requirements for championship titles in that country, would fill a small book. But to give a general idea of why it is more difficult, and therefore more impressive for a dog to gain a title in England than in the United States, a short explanation is in order.

Our American point system for championship is based entirely

Some of Colonel and Mrs. Wingfield Digby's Keeshonds. Sherborne Castle, Dorset.

The 1925 *Dutch Barge Dog Club's* inaugural meeting. In center, Mrs. Wingfield Digby, president, with Ch. Bartel van Zaandam.

on the number of "class" dogs over which a dog has won. In these classes the dog competes with its peers in age and attainment. In England, however, "challengers" for titles are judged in direct competition with champions of record, as well as on their own merits.

To earn a British championship requires receiving three Challenge Certificates under different judges, and at designated "Championship Shows" where CC's are offered for specific breeds. This is not as simple as it may seem. For one thing, all shows are not championship shows for all breeds. Furthermore, CC's for dogs and bitches are *not awarded unless in the judge's written opinion, the quality of the particular animal warrants a CC.* The awards are often withheld.

Title-holders of record are entered in shows in an effort to add more of the coveted Challenge Certificates to their records. But there is no separate class for champions in Great Britain. Champions must be entered in the Open Classes for each sex along with the class entries. Thus, there is no differentiation between the title-holders and non-title-holders in Open class. The winners of the Open and the winners of the other classes compete for the Dog and Bitch CC's (Best of Breed and Best of Opposite Sex). In other words, to win either of the CC's—in dogs or in bitches—requires winning over the champions present in the breed.

As can be readily seen, the British procedure is a definite factor in maintaining a high level of quality in new champions and therefore contributes to breed improvement. Perhaps we in America should consider adopting some of the English requirements for English bench show titles in order to make American championships more meaningful than they are at present.

When the *Dutch Barge Dog Club* was founded in 1925 with Mrs. Digby president, 25 of the breed were registered in England. The next year, the club's name was changed to *The Keeshond Club,* and its first Specialty Show was held in 1933. A second club, *The North of England Keeshond Club* was formed in 1936 under the presidency of Mr. R. Siddall, and both clubs have been active ever since.

In 1929, the first Keeshond completed a championship. It was Baroness Burton's Dochfour Hendrik, bred by Mrs. Digby, sired by her German import, Bartel Van Zaandam. Ch. Hendrik's seven CC's were quite an accomplishment. Mrs. Digby's homebred Gesina Van Zaandam (also by Bartel) was the first bitch to finish, and Gesina's

Miss Beverly's "Kees", bred in Holland. The first shaded sable *Overweight Pomeranian* or Keeshond shown in England.

dam, Breda, was a descendant of Mrs. Digby's original Dutch imports. The first bitch champion was Miss A. H. Kay's Tiptoes. Among winners sired by Ch. Hendrik, Ch. Bingo (ex Darkie of Hyver) became a notable stud. Bingo had been won as a puppy by Mrs. Parker Rhodes in a raffle.

Of the 68 different Kees which received one or more CC's up to 1938, 15 were Van Zaandams. Outstanding among them were Mrs. Digby's owner-bred Ch. Konstanz van Zaandam, who won 11 "tickets" (as CC's are called by British exhibitors), and her Ch. Fina van Zaandam, with 5 CC's to her credit—a prelude to the long record of champions bred-owned-and-handled by Mrs. Digby. Van Zaandam exports also contributed greatly to the establishment of the breed in South Africa in the late 1950s.

As a tribute to Mrs. Digby for her dedicated service to the breed for nearly sixty years, a reception in her honor was held in England in 1962. Among the many honors bestowed upon her by admirers, Mrs. Digby was made an honorary life member of the Keeshond Club of Great Britain, the North of England Keeshond Club, the Keeshond Club of South Africa, and the Keeshond Club of America, and received the American club's Medal of Honor.

In 1969, Mrs. Digby published her memoirs in England. This charmingly written little book by Gwendolyn Wingfield-Digby gives an interesting picture of country life in England, starting shortly after the turn of the 20th century, and is appropriately entitled *"My Life with Keeshonden"*.

After Mrs. Alice Gatacre came from the province of Guelderland in Holland to reside in England around 1928, she imported several Kees from Germany for her Guelder Kennel in Devonshire. Among them were Ado and Flora von Thierlstein, and their dam, Ada von Thierlstein, who whelped Guelder Geron, Ginkel and Gonda while in British quarantine. From them were produced many prominent Guelder Kees which became foundation stock for early British, American, and Canadian breeders. Ado von Thierlstein was the third English champion, and sired Dochfour Jasper, bred by Mrs. W. L. McCandlish (ex her Dochfour Juanita). Lady Burton exported Jasper to Mr. Irving Florsheim in the United States, where in 1932 he became the first dog to win in Keeshond classes in the Westminster Kennel Club show at New York City. Guelder Aga was the first Keeshond trained as a Guide for the Blind in Great Britain.

Baroness Burton's Ch. Dochfour Hendrik, the
first British champion, 1929. (Hendrik van
Zaandam ex Ch. Gesina van Zaandam). Breeder,
Mrs. Digby.

Mrs. Digby's Ch. Bartel van Zaandam (German registered
name, Billo von der Maiblume), the second English champion, 1930.

Ch. Fina van Zaandam, a champion bitch of the early 1930s. Bred and owned by Col. and Mrs. Wingfield Digby.

Ch. Simonius van Zaandam (Ravensdown Chefke ex Mootze of Kynaston). Owners, Col. and Mrs. Digby.

Mrs. Digby's owner-bred Ch. Konstanz van Zaandam (Karel van Zaandam ex Kenau van Zaandam). Sherborne Castle in background. Woodcut by Helen R. Lock.

Ch. Guelder Silvia, bred by Mrs.
Alice Gatacre. Mrs. E. Smith, owner.

Guelder Geron, wh. 1929 ex German-bred Ada van Thierlstein while in British
quarantine. Importer, Mrs. Gatacre.

Mrs. Alice Gatacre's Ch. Ado van Thierlstein, Guelder Geron, Dietz von der Graftschaft Mors and Guelder Canterbury Bell. *Our Dogs* (England), 1937.

Above, German Ch. Dago am Ziel at 7 months. Owner, Dr. Manger of Regensburg. Right, Dago am Ziel's granddaughter and great-granddaughter, Ada von Thierlstein and Guelder Adorata. Owner, Mrs. Gatacre.

The Evenlode family in 1935. In front, Ch. Halunke and Gijsbrecht. Rear,
l. to r., Ch. Hagedorn, Jemima (5 weeks), Busta of Hyver, Ch. Furstin,
Dorcas and Prestbury Greta.

Ch. Wagtail of Evenlode, son
of Ch. Tom Tit of Evenlode.
Owner, Miss O. M. Hastings.

Ch. Major of Broadcliffe, wh.
1941 (Hendrik of Ravensknowle
ex Queen of Tufton). Breeder,
Mrs. I. Newbold.

Mrs. Gatacre's efforts, in 1931, to have the all-white and all-black varieties recognized by The Keeshond Club along with the gray-to-black shaded form, were unsuccessful, and led to her resignation from the club.

A zealous breeder, fancier, and writer, Mrs. Gatacre's pamphlets and magazine articles were outstanding in providing the public with knowledge of the Keeshond, and thus advancing its progress in her adopted country. In addition, she provided an important legacy to English-speaking Keeshond owners in her authoritative book, *The Keeshond*, published in London in 1938. This great classic has been the only comprehensive work devoted exclusively to the breed, but unfortunately has long been out of print.

A striking instance of the fellowship and generosity of unknown dog fanciers on the other side of the world occurred in 1960 in connection with the Gatacre book. Mrs. P. C. Baillie, a Samoyed breeder in New Zealand, wrote me she had read in one of my Keeshond columns in America's *Popular Dogs* magazine that *"The Keeshond"* was almost unobtainable, and offered to send me copies which belonged to her and a friend. On her part, Mrs. Baillie merely expressed interest in receiving copies of Popular Dogs' *Visualization of the Dog Standards*. Her concern for the interests of Keeshond owners in America enabled me to present copies of Mrs. Gatacre's book to local Keeshond clubs for loan to their members.

Miss Osmunda Hastings and her Evenlode Kennel have been famous for consistently contributing top quality Kees to the breed's development and history in both England and America for over 35 years.

Miss Hastings' original bitch, Busta of Hyver, was by Mrs. Digby's Alli von der Sternwarts from Germany, ex Fenna van Zaandam. The mating of Busta to Mrs. Gatacre's imported Cely von Jura de Witt produced Dorcas of Evenlode, a great brood bitch, who founded Evenlode's fame. Bred to Ch. Bingo, Dorcas whelped an outstanding trio of champions in 1934: Eng. and Am. Ch. Halunke of Evenlode (9 CC's) ; his sister, Eng. Ch. Hagedorn of Evenlode (10 CC's) ; and Am. Ch. Herzog of Evenlode. From Hagedorn came Chs. Liebling and Lehmeister of Evenlode.

When Mrs. Richard Fort (later Mrs. Jere Collins) first left England to temporarily live in America, she took Halunke, Herzog and other Kees with her to establish her Van Sandar Kennel in the States. As a show dog and stud, Herzog proved to be an important factor in establishing the breed on the East Coast of the United States. He won the first Keeshond Club of America Specialty, and was the first Keeshond to win a C.D. Obedience title in either England or America. He was the grandsire and double great-grandsire of the illustrious American-bred winner and sire of 25 American champions, Ch. Wynstraat's Kerk. Another son of Dorcas, Am. Ch. Gerolf of Evenlode (sired by Ch. Konstanz van Zaandam), was exported to Dr. and Mrs. Henry Jarrett in Pennsylvania, who were leading founders of The Keeshond Club in the United States.

Dorcas' sister, Diana, bred to the Dutch import Black Bock, produced Ch. Furstin of Evenlode, a winner of 7 CC's and dam of Ch. Ludwig of Evenlode. Just before declaration of World War II, Ch. Liebling was bred to the Dutch import Dietz von der Graftschaft Mors, and their grandson, Pieter of Evenlode became a prominent progenitor of post-war Kees.

When bred to Dochfour Edrick, Dorcas whelped Ch. Lucinda of Evenlode, the dam of Eng. and Am. Ch. Tom Tit of Evenlode. Tom Tit was exported to Mr. and Mrs. Kenneth Fitzpatrick in California, where—in the early 1950s—he was a topflight show winner and stud. Before his exportation, Tom Tit was mated to Unity of Evenlode, who produced Wren of Evenlode, the mother of the well-known brothers, Chs. Young Tom and Young Geron of Evenlode, from whom many of today's prominent British dogs are descended. Wren also whelped Am. Ch. Amanda of Evenlode, who was by Ch. Verschansing of Vorden, and was sent to Mrs. Richard Koehne's Van Ons Kennel in Long Island, N. Y. Ch. Amanda distinguished herself in the 1950s as the dam of five American champions. Am. Ch. Emissory of Evenlode went to Mrs. Gwen Worley in Texas, where he had 13 champion get.

In England, Ch. Tom Tit also sired Ch. Wagtail of Evenlode, whose daughter Ch. Zelda of Evenlode was one of the most beautiful bitches the author has ever seen. Bred to Ch. Young Tom of Evenlode, Zelda produced one of the greatest English studs, Ch. Big Bang of Evenlode, who sired nine British and three U. S. champions. Big Bang's American title-winning sons were: Mr. Kenneth Fitzpatrick's 1958 record-making Ch. Vangabang of Vorden; Mr. and Mrs. Carl Gettig's Ch. Vereeren of Vorden, winner of three Keeshond Club of America Specialties and a Best in Show over 3,180 dogs, and a top-

Ch. Furstin of Evenlode, a prominent bitch winner, 1934–37. (By Dutch-bred Black Bock ex Diana of Evenlode). Breeder-owner: Miss O. Hastings.

Miss Hastings' owner-bred Ch. Liebling of Evenlode, wh. 1937. (Guelder Cinders ex Ch. Hagedorn of Evenlode).

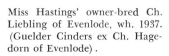

Miss Hastings' Ch. Zelda of Evenlode (Ch. Wagtail of Evenlode ex Verteerbaar of Vorden).

Ch. Big Bang of Evenlode (Ch. Young Tom of Evenlode ex Ch. Zelda of Evenlode), a top ranking stud 1957–65.

Dorcas of Evenlode (Cely von Jura de Wit ex Busta of Hyver), wh. 1930. Bred and owned by Miss Hasting.

Ch. Young Tom of Evenlode
(Ch. Rayvalen Geron of Grovelyn ex Wren of Evenlode), wh.
1951. Breeder-owner, Miss Hastings.

Miss Hastings' Ch. Evenlode
Monarch of Merrybelle, wh.
1958. Top winning Keeshond in
England, 1962 and 1963. (By Ch.
Randalone of Rhinevale ex Ch.
Rondina of Rhinevale). Breeder,
Mr. C. T. Merry.

Mrs. I. M. Tucker's owner-bred
Ch. Verschansing of Vorden (Ch.
Major of Broadcliffe ex Vyand
of Vorden), wh. 1947.

quality stud of the 1960s; and Can. Ch. Sinterklaas Brave Nimrod, obtained from Canada in 1966 by Ruttkay Kennels, for use as a stud.

Ch. Big Bang has an added claim to fame as a grandsire of Miss Hastings' Ch. Evenlode Monarch of Merrybelle, who was by Mrs. Denis Emerson's Ch. Randalone of Rhinevale ex Ch. Rondine of Rhinevale, bred by Mr. G. T. Merry in 1958. Monarch's sensational records included 17 CC's, plus Bests in Show at West of England Ladies Kennel Society's·Show (England's largest outdoor event) and at Ladies Kennel Association (biggest one-day show in the country) in 1962. Monarch also won the Keeshond Club Championship Shows in 1962 and 1963, and took four Bests in Show at Open Shows and three Reserve BIS.

The achievements of Miss Hastings and her Evenlode Kees will forever hold a top place of honor in the breed on both sides of the Atlantic.

One of the objectives of Mrs. Irene Tucker, breeder of the illustrious *of Vorden* Kees, was to never have more than a half-dozen adults, so that each one was a household companion.

From Mrs. Gatacre in 1935, Mrs. Tucker obtained Guelder Vixen, a puppy who in due course was mated to Guelder Ado, and whelped one puppy bitch, Valerie—the first of the Vordens. Valerie became the dam of Vandyke of Vorden, who was best exhibit at the first two breed shows held after World War II, judged respectively by Miss Hastings and Mrs. Wingfield Digby.

Vandyke sired many champions. Among them was Miss Hastings' homebred Eng. and Am. Ch. Tom Tit of Evenlode. Vandyke was also the direct ancestor of Mrs. Tucker's renowned trio of Best in Show winning champions: Verschansing of Vorden (4 CC's); Verrukkelijk (10 CC's); and Verpoozing of Vorden, whelped in 1947 ex Vyand of Vorden and sired by Ch. Major of Broadcliffe. Another champion daughter of Ch. Major was Ch. Vrijster of Vorden (ex Vrijgeleide of Vorden). The sire and dam of Ch. Major, who is back of so many British-bred Kees, were Hendrick of Ravensnowle and Queen of Tufton.

Ch. Verchansing of Vorden was a great stud. Ch. Verrukkelijk's daughter, Verteerbaar of Vorden was the dam of Ch. Zelda of Evenlode, who produced Ch. Big Bang of Evenlode.

In 1952, Vorden Meg of Meadowrock, by Afrik of Willowden ex Zeelands Stormcloud, joined the Vorden family. Meg soon won her title, and went on to collect a total of nine CC's. Bred to Ch. Verschansing of Vorden, in her first litter she whelped the history-making bitch, Ch. Volkrijk of Vorden. Volkrijk shattered all breed records by collecting 24 CC's at 25 successive championship shows, and was best of all breeds in 18 of them. But in 1957, she topped her sensational career with the greatest triumph of all. Ch. Volkrijk of Vorden, handled as always by Mrs. Tucker, won the award of Supreme Champion at Crufts' in London, over what was a world-record entry at the time of 12,676 (made up by 6,562 dogs). In the same year, she was also Best in Show at the Ayr Championship Show.

Ch. Volkrijk's achievements were not confined to the ring. Her first litter was by Ch. Big Bang of Evenlode and included Ch. Volk-rad of Vorden (4 CC's) and Am. Ch. Vangabang of Vorden. Vangabang was exported to Kenneth Fitzpatrick in the States, where he won the 1958 Quakers Oats Award for the largest number of Group First awards by any dog of any breed in the western part of the country.

A daughter of Ch. Verschansing ex Aura of Goss was Ch. Veraura of Vorden, the winner of 13 CC's and 15 Bests of all breeds. Veraura won her first ticket when $7\frac{1}{2}$ months old, was a champion at 10 months, and received her last CC at five years of age. She was the dam of many British winners, including Ch. Vanderveer of Ven and Ch. Voljasmijn of Vorden.

Am. Ch. Virginia of Vorden, a daughter of Veraura's by Ch. Young Geron of Evenlode, was a foundation bitch for Mr. and Mrs. John A. Lafore's Chantwood Kennel in Pennsylvania, where Virginia produced six of Chantwood's 17 champions. Two others came from breeding their Ch. Ruttkay Secret Love, a Ch. Verschansing granddaughter, to their Am. Ch. Voljester of Vorden, imported from England.

Ch. Vorden Good Guard of Evenlode, a son of Ch. Verschansing out of Double Diamond of Evenlode, took five Best in Show awards. His first litter, which was out of Vrivolity of Vorden, added two more title winners to Vorden's impressive records. They were Eng. and Am. Ch. Vaalsmeer of Vorden (5 CC's) and Eng. Ch. Verkrijgen of Vorden. Good Guard was also the grandsire of Am. Ch. Vereeren of Vorden exported to Mr. and Mrs. Gettig in the United States. Though seldom shown, Vereeren made a great name for himself as a show dog, and as a stud whose excellence was passed on to his numerous champion sons and daughters, and their progeny.

69

The pedigrees of many prominent Kees in America show that there was a considerable amount of collaboration between Miss Hastings and Mrs. Tucker in respect to the breeding programs of their Evenlode and Vorden Kennels. In fact, the pedigrees of these great breeders' dogs are a veritable Who's Who of famous Keeshonds. It was a serious loss to the breed when, in 1963, Mrs. Tucker discontinued raising Kees.

A visit by Mr. and Mrs. Fred Greenwood to see Mrs. Tucker's Keeshonds in 1943 led to the founding of the Greenwoods' celebrated Wistonia Kennel in the north of England. They went home with five-month-old Vandyquette of Vorden, bred by Mrs. Hudson out of her Vega of Vorden and sired by Vandyke of Vorden. A few months later, Mrs. Tucker offered to show Vandyquette at a local show, where she won three first prizes, and so the Greenwoods got the "show bug".

On the recommendation of Mrs. Doreen Anderson of the Kultz Kennel, Vandyquette's first Wistonia litter was by Pieter of Evenlode. But the one puppy kept for breeding was killed by a car. Unable to buy back any of the littermates, the Greenwoods purchased Zandi van Zaandam from Mrs. Wingfield Digby and bred Zandi to Aalik of Wistonia, a male in Vandyquette's litter. From this mating came Worthy of Wistonia, the start of the Wistonia line. He sired seven champions, a record at the time, and according to Mrs. Greenwood, it is to Worthy that the kennel owes all of its success.

The foundation stock behind Wistonia's record-making Kees in England, and the kennel's many exports with spectacular winning records in America, came from various British breeders. Anna of Vanloen, by Loen Lancer ex Silver Jubilee, was bred by Mr. Dunwell. Anna became a champion and the dam of Flakkee Kennel's imported Eng. and Am. Ch. Waarborg of Wistonia, whose sire was Worthy of Wistonia. And Vallei of Vorden was by Vandyke of Vorden out of Mrs. L. Wright's Mooe Maesga. Wistonia's final purchase was Mr. and Mrs. J. Fryer's Hecate of Muirville. Hecate won her title, and in her litter by Worthy, produced Am. Ch. Allendale of Wistonia (exported to Mr. William Dick in the United States) and Eng. Ch. Wazelaine of Wistonia (dam of five British champions—another record).

In one litter, Ch. Wazelaine had Eng. and Am. Ch. Wylco of Wistonia, and in her next were Eng. Chs. Wynkanton, Wendhausen,

70

Ch. Volkrijk of Vorden (b), wh. 1954. First Keeshond to become Supreme Champion (Best in Show) at Crufts—1957, 6,652 dogs. (Ch. Verschansing of Vorden ex Ch. Vorden Meg of Meadow Rock). Breeder-owner, Mrs. I. M. Tucker.

Wayston and Wazzi of Wistonia, all sired by Ch. Winchell of Wistonia. Ch. Winchell was by Worthy ex Thelma of Grovelyn, and was bred by Mrs. O. Davies. He joined the Greenwoods' kennel as a puppy, and sired 11 champions, thus breaking the record established by his sire, Worthy.

It was not until the resumption of Championship Shows after World War II that the Greenwoods could compete with Kees from all over the country. Between 1947 and 1950 they finished seven champions, two of which—Eng. and Am. Chs. Whimsy and Waarborg of Wistonia—were exported to Mrs. Porter Washington's Flakkee Kennel in California.

During the next eight years, the Greenwoods also sent to Flakkee: Eng. and Am. Chs. Wrona, Wylco, and Wrocky (Wylco's son) —all with Wistonia suffix; Aristocrat of Dorel, bred by Mrs. W. W. Holmes; and Am. Ch. Worrall of Wistonia. As related in detail in Chapter 5, the Greenwoods' exports to Flakkee Kennel swept through Western American shows to make dramatic new national records for Kees as Group and Best in Show winners, and were the basis for Flakkee Kennel's outstanding success.

Eng. Am. and Can. Ch. Wrocky of Wistonia became internationally famous under the Washingtons' ownership. His 18 Bests in Show, 32 Group Firsts, and 35 Bests of Breed in the 36 times he was shown in 1956/57 topped the triumphs of all other Kees in America until his line-bred American-born grandson, Ch. Flakkee Sweepstakes, went on to spectacular new heights in 1967 and 1968.

Bred to the author's imported Eng. and Am. Ch. Wot-A-Gal of Wistonia, Ch. Wrocky sired Ch. Nederlan Winston of Wistonia, whose line-bred grandson, Ch. Nederlan Herman v. Mack broke all Best in Show and Group records achieved by an American-bred Kees prior to 1967, and won eight Eastern Specialty shows.

Wrocky is pictured on page 140 as model in the pictorial depiction of the breed standard. This depiction has appeared in the *Visualization of the Dog Standards* (published by *Popular Dogs,* and used here with their permission) , and in the Keeshond Club of America's breed pamphlet.

Other Wistonia exports were acquired by Mr. and Mrs. A. C. Kaufmann in California, Mrs. E. C. Stoodley in Pennsylvania, Mrs. Murray Woronor in Texas, and Mrs. McGregor in Canada.

Mrs. Tucker's Ch. Vorden Good Guard of Evenlode (Ch. Verschansing of Vorden ex Double Diamond of Evenlode), wh. 1959.

Mrs. Tucker's Ch. Veraura of Vorden (Ch. Verschansing of Vorden ex Aura of Goss), wh. 1955.

Ch. Volkrad of Vorden (Ch. Big Bang of Evenlode ex Ch. Volkrijk of Vorden), wh. 1956. Bred and owned by Mrs. Tucker.

The Greenwoods bred or owned 38 English champions, plus 19 American and 4 Canadian titlists—an impressive record in itself. In addition, for 12 years (11 consecutively) Wistonia won the Norton Rose Bowl, emblematic of the top winning kennel of the year. For seven straight years, Wistonia's studs received the Ch. Bingo Bowl for Top Stud of the Year, and seven times the Dorcas of Evenlode Challenge Cup for Top Brood Bitch was awarded to the kennel's bitches.

In 1964, Mr. and Mrs. Greenwood and their Keeshonds left England to live in the United States. Before their departure, the North of England Keeshond Club held a dinner in their honor where they received gifts and the following citation:

"Presented to Nan and Fred Greenwood by the members of the Club as a token of esteem and gratitude for their unselfish service to the Club and devotion to the breed during the years 1943–1964."

Not long after taking residence in Pennsylvania, Mr. Greenwood's sad death robbed the breed of a great breeder. But his equally distinguished partner, Nan Greenwood, has carried on the renowned Wistonia traditions in California. Her Eng. Ch. Whiplash of Wistonia, a British Group winner and sire of one English and two South African champions, soon became an American champion, and sired 10 American title winners. The great achievements of Wistonia Kees in England and the United States, and of the descendants, speak for themselves.

Mrs. Jere Collins' kennel has been literally international right from the beginning. It started in England when Mrs. Collins was Mrs. Richard Fort. It was then moved to Pleasantville, N.Y. in 1935, and her van Sandar Kennel's British-bred Keeshonds and their American-born progeny played vital roles in the breed's development in the United States. After Mr. and Mrs. Collins' marriage, and the end of World War II, they returned to England where they re-established their kennel as *Ven*.

Young Geron of Evenlode was then bought as a puppy from Miss Hastings and was the first of many champions finished or bred by Ven Kennel. Young Geron's mating to Mrs. Tucker's Ch. Veraura of Vorden produced Ch. Vanderveer of Vorden, who became Ven's foundation bitch.

Eng. Am. Ch. Whiplash of Wistonia, wh. 1961 in England. (Wanjohe of Wistonia ex Winlunde of Wistonia). Breeders: Mr. and Mrs. Fred Greenwood (Wistonia Kennel), England. Owner, Mrs. N. Greenwood (Wistonia Kennel), California.

Mr. and Mrs. J. R. Collins' Ch. Vanderveer of Vorden, her daughter—Tassle of Ven, and Tassle's daughter, Ch. Vivandiere of Ven.

Ch. Young Geron of Evenlode (Ch. Rayvalen Geron of Grovelyn ex Wren of Evenlode), wh. 1951. Breeder, Miss Hastings. Owners, Mr. and Mrs. J. R. Collins, Ven Kennels.

75

Ch. Saskia of Ven (ex Vanessa of Ven), the dam of Am. Ch. Waloon of Ven, exported to America.

Ch. Vivandiere of Ven (Commandant of Duroya ex Tassle of Ven).

Ch. Aunt Susan of Ven (Ch. Big Bang of Evenlode ex Ch. Vanderveer of Ven). Bred and owned by Mr. and Mrs. Collins.

Ch. Vanderveer was bred to Ch. Big Bang of Evenlode on two occasions. In the first litter were Ch. Berryvale Smug of Evenlode, Ch. Dutch Uncle of Ven and Tassle of Ven, who took one CC and two Reserves. Tassle in turn, became the mother of Ch. Vivandiere of Ven, who, as the dam of Ch. Saskia of Ven, became the maternal granddam of a dog exported to America in the 1960s, Am. Ch. Waloon of Ven. The second Vanderveer/Big Bang litter produced the well-known Ch. Aunt Susan of Ven.

When Am. Ch. Ruttkay Moerdaag was imported from America by Ven Kennel in 1963, he was the first American-bred Keeshond to go to England. Moerdaag became the sire of two champions: Ch. Belle Blond of Berryvale (out of Ch. Berryvale Smug), and Ch. Welford Lucky, the 1968 Best of Breed at Crufts. (Lucky's dam was Welford Ina, owned by Miss Glover). In line with Mr. and Mrs. Collins' efforts to contribute to the breed's progress, they have also imported the two Dutch puppies named Brenda and Arnhem Immertrouw from the Sigelinski line.

Mr. and Mrs. Collins' popularity as judges has included assignments on the Continent and in Scandinavian countries. They were also enthusiastically acclaimed for their judging of the 1968 Keeshond Club of Delaware Valley Specialty in Pennsylvania, which drew 182 entries, made up by 141 Kees.

The success of Mrs. Denis Emerson's carefully limited breeding program for raising her Rhinevale Kennel Keeshonds is notable in several respects. When, by chance, as a teen-ager, she saw the dogs in Miss Hastings' Evenlode Kennel, she became permanently smitten by the beauty and character of the breed and the desire to raise them. But her youth and World War II intervened.

The first and *only* Keeshond Mr. and Mrs. Emerson have ever bought was Tabitha of Evenlode, a member of Miss Hastings' first post-war litter in 1945. All nine generations of Rhinevale Kees have descended from Tabitha.

There are Rhinevale winners in many countries. Ch. Rapunzel of Rhinevale was in the third litter raised by Mrs. Emerson, who has said: "We owe everything to Rapunzel—looks and wonderful character." Rapunzel's grandson, Ch. Randalone of Rhinevale (a singleton), sired the first Finnish champion, Ralanda of Rhinevale. From this line came French Ch. Repartee of Rhinevale, the first Keeshond

Ch. Rapunzel of Rhinevale (b.) and grandson, Ch. Randalone of Rhinevale. Breeder-owner, Mrs. Denis Emerson.

Mrs. Emerson's owner-bred Ch. Robinella of Rhinevale (Ch. Rahida of Rhinevale ex Ch. Robertina of Rhinevale), top winning bitch in England for 1969.

Can. and Am. Ch. Rugosa of Rhinevale (Ch. Rahida of Rhinevale ex Ch. Raphaella of Rhinevale), top winning bitch in the United States for 1969. Bred by Mrs. D. Pumfrey, England. Owned by Mrs. E. K. Olafson, Canada.

to win Best in Show in France, and Int. Ch. Rampant of Rhinevale, who became the top winning Scandinavian stud dog.

Mrs. Emerson's exports to Mrs. E. K. Olafson in Canada, Can. Ch. Racassius of Rhinevale and Am and Can. Ch. Rugosa of Rhinevale, soon made their mark in the United States. Ch. Rugosa was the 1969 top-winning show bitch, and several of her puppies gained American titles in short order.

Ch. Robinella of Rhinevale was Best in Show in the 1967 British Keeshond Club Championship Show and the 1969 top winning bitch in England. Also in 1969, Mrs. Emerson with Ch. Duroya Roleander of Rhinevale took Reserve Best in Show at Windsor in over 8,000 entries.

In addition to having judged the breed in England since 1952, Mrs. Emerson officiated in Sweden in 1969, and early that year was invited to judge the 1970 Keeshond Club of America Specialty.

Other English breeders whose kennel names are known for their exports, which became winners and producers of winners in the United States, are: Mrs. P. F. Parkes, Sinterklaas; Mrs. E. M. Smyth, Waakzaam; and Mrs. E. E. Woodiwiss, Duroya.

The history of the Keeshond in the 20th century clearly shows how greatly the breed as a whole, and American fanciers in particular, are indebted to British breeders, and always will be.

79

Mr. Carl Hinderer with two of the first American-bred litter, 1929. Bred by Mr. Hinderer.

Wachter Schwartz, wh. 1924, one of Mr. Carl H. Hinderer's first imports to Baltimore, Maryland in 1926, which led to the breed's registration as Keeshonden by the American Kennel Club in 1930. (Breeder, Carl Schwartz, Germany.)

5

The Keeshond
in the United States

AS previously noted, the development of the Keeshond in America, with few exceptions, is based on imports from England, which were in turn the product of British importations from Holland and Germany.

The progress of a breed depends on many factors. High on the list of these factors are the successful efforts of breeders to maintain the breed's correct temperament, to raise quality dogs in relation to the official standard of excellence prescribed for the breed, and to exhibit dogs of merit in the rings.

The official yardsticks in America for appraisal of the overall quality of a breed, or of its individual members and kennels, are the number of American Kennel Club championship titles completed, the records of dogs and bitches as producers of champions, and the totals of wins achieved, notably all-breed Bests in Show, Group firsts and placements, and Specialty Show Bests of Breed. (See Chapter 12 on Showing.)

There are some other measures which, though unofficial, have also become important. The annual Phillips Ratings awards points for each Best in Show, Group First, or Group placement win in accordance with the number of dogs over whom the win was scored. The Quaker Oats Awards, also presented annually, previously honored the one dog of any breed in each of four sections of the country that had won the most Group Firsts during the previous year. Beginning in 1967, this was changed to honor the one dog of each Group, regardless of geographical location, that had won the most Group Firsts during the previous year. These ratings and awards are therefore significant, and have become highly prized recognitions of achievement in the rings.

The show success of the Keeshond in this country has been phenomenal in proportion to the number annually registered since 1930. This indicates that fortunately for the breed, emphasis has been on breeding for quality rather than quantity or financial gain. But commercialism and large scale "puppy-mill" operations in Kees are a seriously increasing problem.

Not apparent from official or other records is the fact that most of the top-ranking show Kees have been house-pets whose show careers were a sideline to their main roles in their owners' homes. Comparatively few outstanding winners have been produced or shown by commercial kennels. And kennel names are used by breeders to identify and register the dogs they raise, whether the "kennel" is conducted on a small, personal basis or on a large scale.

The Keeshond was first introduced in the United States in the East and Midwest, and about six years later, on the West Coast. As a result, the preponderance of activity in the breed has been based mainly in these areas.

In order to present chronological accounts of owners and their dogs in the respective areas, this chapter has been divided accordingly. It has also been written with a view to showing the amount of inter-relationship there was in many Keeshonden who have contributed prominently to the breed throughout America.

The East and Midwest

Since the first Keeshonden registered by the American Kennel Club (1930) were brought here in 1926, so much has been achieved by so many importers, breeders, and exhibitors in the United States, that it is only possible to touch on the highlights.

The efforts and experiences of Carl Hinderer as a young man and former citizen of Stuttgart, Germany, are outstanding, because they led to the official recognition of the breed in America. Enthused by seeing Miss J. G. van der Blom's Dutch Keeshond-Spitz at the 1921 Stuttgart show, when he was himself 21 years of age, Mr. Hinderer obtained a puppy in 1922. The next year he emigrated to Baltimore, Maryland, but had to leave his dog behind. In 1926, after he imported four pedigreed Wolfsspitz from Germany, he learned that the breed was not recognized by the American Kennel Club under any name. But young Mr. Hinderer tackled the problem with determination.

The next four years involved his continuous correspondence with the *Verein fur Deutsche Spitz* (German Spitz Club) in Germany, and the American Kennel Club, and many trips to the AKC offices in New York to confer with officials, and to show Wachter Schwartz, one of his imports, to the AKC's president.

Mr. Hinderer joined the Maryland Kennel Club and informally exhibited his dogs in the Baltimore area and at the Club's 1928 and 1929 shows. He found that though the dogs created a great deal of favorable comment, the name "Wolfsspitz" did not appeal to the public. Finally, in 1930, his efforts resulted in the AKC's recognition of the breed as Keeshonden, classified under Group 6, Non-Sporting Dogs. The first 17 of the breed registered were Carl Hinderer's imports and their puppies. Shortly afterward, however, distemper took all but three of his 20 dogs, and this tragedy put an end to his breeding.

Mr. Hinderer judged Keeshonden as honorary judge at the 1933 Maryland KC show, but after 1934 he did not attend another show until the Club's 1965 event. There he met Mrs. Lois McNamara, a founder and former president of the Capital Keeshond Club, and Mrs. Carl Gettig, the Keeshond Club of America columnist for the AKC's *Pure-Bred Dogs—American Kennel Gazette,* to whom he related his experiences. In recognition of his important role in the

Guelder Chinchilla, early import. Breeder, Mrs. Alice Gatacre, England. Owner, Mr. Irving Florsheim.

Mr. Florsheim's imported Dochfour Jasper. Breeder, Mrs. McCandish, England.

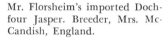

Am. Ch. Dochfour Hans, the first American-bred champion. Breeder-owner, Mr. Florsheim.

breed in the United States, Mr. Hinderer was elected a life member of the Capital Keeshond Club, received the Keeshond Club of America's Medal of Honor, and was made Honorary Member of the *Verein fur Deutsche Spitz.*

Mr. and Mrs. Irving Florsheim were active, early breeders. They established their Red Top Kennel on their estate near Chicago in 1930, basing it on imports from England: Lady Burton's Dochfour Jasper, bred by Mrs. McCandlish; Mrs. Alice Gatacre's Guelder Kennel's Chinchilla, Petrucia, Primrose, and Silver Witch; Mrs. Wingfield Digby's Taal, Karon and other Van Zaandams, and Miss O. M. Hastings' Geraard of Evenlode. The Florsheims' Dochfour Hans (sired by Dochfour Jasper ex Guelder Chinchilla) became the first American-bred champion. The breed was introduced in California when, in 1932, Mr. Florsheim sent a puppy bitch to Mrs. Kenneth Fitzpatrick, who registered her as Guelder Fitzpatrick, and started the famous Van Fitz Kennel in Encino.

The Florsheims' activities continued for about eight years, and when *The Keeshond Club,* as it was first named, was formed in the United States in 1935, Mrs. Florsheim was its first president.

Another early breeder was Mrs. H. C. House in Farmington, Connecticut, and her imports of Mrs. Gatacre's Guelder Child of the Mist, Grey Dawn, Pearly King and Seamist are in many American pedigrees.

Mrs. Henry Jarrett of Philadelphia did not raise many litters, but she was so keen about Kees after obtaining British-bred Am. Ch. Gerolf of Evenlode from Miss Hastings that she and Dr. Jarrett contributed greatly to the breed in many ways. She was a leading member of The Keeshond Club as its first secretary-treasurer, and then president for several years after Mrs. Florsheim's retirement. In 1963, Mrs. Jarrett was made an Honorary Member of the national club.

Mrs. Richard Fort, a British subject, brought her English Van Sandar Kennel to Pleasantville, N.Y. in 1935 on the first of several temporary sojourns in America. Her Kees included her home-bred Black Peter, Lady Cooper's Prestbury Sister, Miss Hastings' Herzog of Evenlode and his brother, Eng. Ch. Halunke of Evenlode. They and Mr. Irving Florsheim's Geraard of Evenlode and Mrs. House's Guelder Pearly King were among the first Kees to become American champions.

Ch. Herzog CD is particularly notable on several counts. Trained and handled by Mrs. Fort, he was the first Keeshond Companion

Am. Ch. Guelder Pearly King. Bred by Mrs. Alice Gatacre, England. Imported in the early 1930s by Mrs. H. C. House, Connecticut.

Am. Ch. Herzog of Evenlode, C.D. and Am. Ch. Black Peter. Herzog, wh. 1934, won the first American Keeshond Club Specialty in 1937, and was the first Keeshond C.D. titlist in the East. Bred by Miss O. M. Hastings, England, and imported by Mrs. Richard Fort.

Dog titlist in the world. In 1937 he won the first Keeshond Specialty in the United States, and Mrs. Fort's owner-bred Anni Van Sander took Winners Bitch at the same event, held with the Ladies Kennel Association of America show in Garden City, Long Island, New York.

Herzog had four Group placings, and sired a number of champions. Through Mrs. Fort's selective line-breeding program, he appears three times in the pedigree of Mrs. Jean Vincent's famous Ch. Wynstraat's Kerk, whelped in 1947. In fact, Herzog sired Mrs. Fort's home-bred Hans Brinker Van Sander, who was Kerk's sire.

Ch. Black Peter also scored in Groups, and in 1936 Ch. Prestbury Sister made history as the first Keeshond bitch to win a Group, and took three other placings. Rare achievements by a female, especially in those early days.

After Mrs. Fort's marriage to Jere Collins, and the end of World War II, Mr. and Mrs. Collins moved from their home in Millbrook, N. Y. to permanently reside in England, where (as already recounted in the chapter on English kennels) their successful breeding was carried on under the *of Ven* suffix.

Starting in 1937, the large number of Kees produced in Ohio for over ten years by the David Holdermans' Holdermere Kennel and Walter B. Garland, can be credited with pioneering the breed in that area. Among the champions bred in New Jersey by Mrs. Annie Adams was the Russell Thompsons' well-known Ch. Dirk Adams. Mrs. Adams was also at one time an Honorary Member of the Keeshond Club.

Other kennel names of the 1940s and 1950s found in Eastern and other Kees' pedigrees include *Bobsno,* owned by Mrs. Edna Hodgson of Pennsylvania; *Knappholme,* owned by the Thomas R. Knapps of New Jersey; Martin Faigley's *Artel* in New York; Louis Todd's *Kingleigh* in Indiana, and William Dick's *Allen-Winden* in New York.

A Christmas gift puppy named Schoon, received by Virginia Liggett when she was in her teens in 1939, was the start of her Nether-Lair Kennel in Massachusetts. (She later married Jack Cowley.) Bred by A. G. Schindler in Connecticut, Schoon's immediate ancestors were Mrs. House's imported Guelder Kees. As a result of his young owner's interest in Obedience training. Schoon became the first Eastern CDX title winner, and completed his UD class work, but not the Tracking Tests which were required in those days for a UD title.

Am. Ch. Prestbury Sister, the first Keeshond bitch Group winner in the United States (1936). Breeder: Lady Cooper, England. Owner: Mrs. Richard Fort (Van Sandar Kennels).

Eng. Am. Ch. Halunke of Evenlode (Eng. Ch. Bingo ex Dorcas of Evenlode), one of the first American champions in the East. Breeder: Miss O. M. Hastings, England. Owner: Mrs. Richard Fort.

Annie Van Sandar, Winners Bitch at the first Keeshond Specialty in the United States, 1937. Breeder-owner: Mrs. Richard Fort.

The first Nether-Lair litter was by Schoon ex Julie Pool, a bitch whose parents were David Van Sandar and Adams Juliana. Flicka de Gyselaer was one of that litter born in 1942, and when bred to Mrs. Vincent's Ch. Wynstraat's Kerk in 1949, Flicka produced Ch. Nether-Lair's Banner de Gyselaer, who became a well-known show dog and stud, owned by the author.

Conwood Kressa and Conwood Adrienne, obtained as brood bitches from Mrs. Lillian O'Connor's Conwood Kennel in Canada, had British Vorden Kees behind them, and with Ch. Brinka v. Elmhurst as stud were original factors in the success of Nether-Lair's breeding program. Though comparatively few Nether-Lair Kees were shown by their purchasers, this fine kennel bred more than 30 champions. Mrs. Cowley's retirement as a breeder in 1964 was a great loss.

Nether-Lair also contributed to the breed's progress through people whose activities in Kees were started or augmented by acquiring Nether-Lair dogs. Mrs. Ralph Porter's Ch. Nether-Lair's Tchortie CD won the 1959 national Specialty. Mrs. Harriet Ovington's Ch. Nether-Lair's Damon de Gyselaer CD, with her home-bred Har-Curt's Hansel (a son of Damon), made up a 1954 Best in Show winning brace, and her Holland Hond's Kennel produced a number of champions.

As a member of the Keeshond Club of America's Board of Directors from 1955 to 1969, Mrs. Ovington's work for the club has been outstanding. She served as treasurer for several years, and during her chairmanship of the Breeder's Ethics Committee, the club's *Breeders' Code of Ethics* was adopted in 1965 as a guide for breeders and owners of Keeshonden. Mrs. Ovington also became the first president of the Heritage Trail Keeshond Club, founded in 1964 in Massachusetts.

The Wynfomeer Kennel in Long Island had its origin in 1940 when, as a young girl, Betty Dunn was given her first Keeshond, Vermont Monte. The Dunn family liked him so much as a pet that in 1944 they purchased Bobsno's Delfzi and bred her to Mrs. Adams' Ch. King Dusky. Miss Dunn raised her first litter in 1946. After Pat's Gay Blade (by Ch. Wynstraat's Schnaaps ex Ch. Floret Adams) was obtained from Mrs. Jean Vincent, Miss Dunn finished his championship in five shows, and trained and handled him to his CDX title. In 1949 and 1950, her Ch. Pat's Gay Blade CDX with a home-bred son, Ch. Pat's Gay Demon CD, brought distinction to the breed as the first Keeshond brace to win the Non-Sporting Group at the Westminster Kennel Club show in New York City. They were also the Best Brace in Group at the important Eastern Dog Club event in Boston in 1950.

By this time, E. J. Cummings III (Miss Dunn's future husband) had bought Mrs. Vincent's Wynstraat's Cover Boy, who was by the Thompsons' Ch. Dirk Adams ex Ch. Wynstraat's Delft. Cover Boy became the first UD Keeshond in the country, a bench champion and member of the Keeshond Club of America's first Obedience team. Miss Dunn with Pat's Gay Blade was also a Team member in 1951. About a year later, Cover Boy and Pat's Gay Blade attended their owners' wedding reception, and Wynfomeer became Mr. and Mrs. Cummings III's kennel name.

Wynstraat's Garry, by Ch. Dirdon's Durk Donder ex Ch. Wynstraat's Delft, bred by Mrs. Vincent, joined Wynfomeer Kennel as a puppy in 1958. Sire of 12 champions, winner of eight Groups and 44 placings, Ch. Garry highlighted his career with Best in Show, as had his American-bred sire (Durk Donder) and grandsire (Ch. Wynstraat's Kerk) before him. Garry also won a Best American-bred in Show award, and with a homebred son, Ch. Wynfomeer's The Royal Lancer, took Best Non-Sporting Brace at Westminster in 1960. The next year the pair went to the top as Best Brace in Show at Westminster. Following his retirement from bench competition, Garry earned his CD in three straight shows. This made him, by a few months, the second dual-titled Best in Show winning Keeshond in the United States. Preceding him to the honor was Mrs. Charles Mulock's Ch. Rikki Van Armel CD, of Colorado, bred by Walter Winkler, and by Ch. Vangabang of Vorden ex Ch. Wilhelmina of Kittridge.

Mr. and Mrs. Cummings III have been active members of the Keeshond Club of America for many years, and in many capacities. In 1965 they were recipients of the *Dog World Award* for their work for the breed, and their initiation and chairmanship of the national club's Puppy Futurity Stake, established in 1963. The Cummings also presented the club with a Futurity Stake Challenge Trophy for Best in Futurity, in memory of Ch. Tassel of Artel, Ch. Van Fitz Hocage, and Ch. Wynstraat's Delft, dams of three generations of BIS Keeshonden.

Ever since Mr. and Mrs. Russell S. Thompson of Long Island

Ch. Wynstraat's Kerk (Ch. Hans Brinker van Sandar ex Ch. Tassel of Artel), wh. 1947, the first American-bred Best in Show winner in the East. Breeder-owner: Wynstraat Kennels (Mrs. Jean Vincent).

Ch. Wynstraat's Garry (Ch. Dirdon's Durk Donder ex Ch. Wynstraat's Delft), wh. 1954, the second Ch. and CD titlist in the United States to win Best in Show, 1961. Breeder: Wynstraat Kennel. Owner: Wynfomeer Kennels (Mr. and Mrs. E. J. Cummings III).

91

bought three-year-old Dirk Adams as a pet from Mrs. Adams' kennel in 1944, they have done a great deal to augment the progress of Keeshonden through their work as officers of the Keeshond Club, as exhibitors, and as judges.

The Thompsons' handsome pet was a grandson of Mrs. Collins' imported Ch. Herzog of Evenlode and a great-grandson of Ch. Black Peter. Handled by Mrs. Thompson throughout his show career, Ch. Dirk Adams was a dominant breed winner in the East. In his long list of wins were Bests of Breed at Westminster in 1944 and 1945, and the national club's Specialties in 1946, 1947 and 1948. Mr. and Mrs. Thompson were chosen by the club's membership to judge the 1958 and 1959 Keeshond Club of America Specialty Shows.

When Mr. and Mrs. Jere Collins returned permanently to England, Mr. and Mrs. Thompson succeeded them as president and secretary-treasurer of the Keeshond Club in America. During the many years in these capacities, the Thompsons' efforts to encourage and assist potential breeders and exhibitors through Club newsletters and personal contacts with Keeshond owners, gave lasting impetus to the breed's development, especially in the East. Mr. Thompson has been an outstanding member of the national breed club's Board of Directors since 1946, and after his resignation from the presidency, was the club's delegate to the American Kennel Club from 1951 to 1963. He again served as president for the year of 1968.

The name and achievements of Mrs. Jean Vincent's numerically small Wynstraat Kennel in Millbrook, N. Y. are outstanding in the breed's eastern history. Mrs. Vincent acquired Mr. and Mrs. Collins' Hans Brinker Van Sandar, who was bred to Wynstraat-owned Ch. Tassel of Artel in 1946. The resulting litter produced the great Ch. Wynstraat's Kerk, whose pedigree includes Chs. Herzog of Evenlode, Cim Van Sander, Bobsno's Sister Dinky, Guelder Gray Cloud and Prestbury Sister.

Surprising as it may now seem, Keeshonden were seldom given a second glance in eastern Group rings before Ch. Kerk's career started in 1948. Fortunately for the breed, Kerk's striking appearance combined with his successful campaigning by Mrs. Vincent, and by A. J. Meshirer as co-owner, paved the way for future Kees' recognition as Group and Best in Show winners. Kerk was the first Keeshond to take Best in Show in the East. In his 154 Bests of Breed, he won 31 Groups, 36 seconds, 24 thirds, 17 fourths, won the Keeshond

First Keeshond brace to top Westminster, 1954:
Ch. Dirdon's Wonder Wander Hocage, CD and
younger brother, Ch. Dirdon's Helder Zwier, CD).
Breeder: Dirdon Kennels (Marjorie P. Cummings.
Owner: Marye E. Picone.

Best in Show brace at Westminster, 1961: Ch.
Wynfomeer's The Royal Lancer and sire, Ch.
Wynstraat's Garry, CD. Owner: Wynfomeer Ken-
nels.

Club of America Specialties from 1949 through 1953, and was BOB at several Westminster shows—a top Eastern record at that time. Mr. and Mrs. Edwin Locke's Ch. Wynstraat's Hydraulic Jack, by Nero van Beau, also did well in Groups.

Ch. Kerk's influence on the breed as sire of 25 champions, and many other good Kees, was as important as his show record. Two of his best-known sons were the author's Ch. Nether-Lair's Banner de Gyselaer, bred by Mrs. Cowley, and Mrs. E. J. Cummings II's owner-bred Ch. Dirdon's Durk Donder, who became prominent show dogs. Ch. Wynstraat's Delft, a litter sister of Kerk, whelped eight champions, and, bred to Durk Donder, produced the BIS-winning Ch. Wynstraat's Garry CD.

Mrs. Vincent deserves great credit for her contributions to the breed through her activities as a breeder, exhibitor, and as secretary of the Keeshond Club of America.

Like many others who became breeders, the author's devotion to Keeshonden was from being "owned by" a puppy. As a beautiful ball of fluff, Winkel bounced into my life in 1941 from a litter raised by Mrs. Marie Byrne in Massachusetts, and was the reason for founding Nederlan Kennel in Connecticut.

The scarcity of the breed in the area and restrictions on travel during World War II, delayed locating a suitable, accessible, stud. Finally, in 1947, Winkel was bred to the Russell Thompson's Ch. Dirk Adams, but the one puppy kept for breeding was killed by a car.

After this tragedy, Nether-Lair's Banner de Gyselaer (by Ch. Wynstraat's Kerk ex Flicka de Gyselaer), bred by Mrs. Cowley in 1949, was obtained by Nederlan from Mr. Harold Vanik. Banner proved to be a good winner in his comparatively few shows, all of which were no farther than 150 miles from home. His 41 BOB included the 1953 national Specialty, Westminster in 1954 and 1956, and he took three Groups and 31 placements. Ch. Banner also sired 12 of the 40 champions bred, sired, or owned by Nederlan Kennel. Among his get was Mrs. Alfred McCormack's owner-bred pet, Ch. Keeshaven's Clown, who won the 1958 Keeshond Club of America Specialty plus a number of Group placements.

Mrs. McCormack's enthusiasm about the "fur-people", as she always called Kees, prompted her giving a unique party in Washington D.C. after the 1958 Capital Keeshond Club Specialty. Engraved

94

Ch. Nether-Lair's Banner de Gyselaer
(Ch. Wynstraat's Kerk ex Flicka de
Gyselaer), wh. 1949. Breeder: Mrs.
Jack Cowley, Nether-Lair Kennel.
Owner: Mrs. J. Whitney Peterson,
Nederlan Kennels.

Ch. Nederlan Winston of Wistonia (Eng. Ch. Wrocky
of Wistonia ex Eng. Am. Ch. Wot-A-Gal of Wistonia),
wh. 1954 in the United States. Breeder: Mrs. Nan
Greenwood, Eng. Owner, Mrs. J. Whitney Peterson.

Am. Can. Ch. Nederlan Herman V. Mack (Ch. Baron Mack of Keeshof
ex Ch. Nederlan Ursa v. Winston), wh. 1959. Breeder: Mrs. J. Whitney
Peterson. Owners: Mr. and Mrs. Emerson P. Hempstead.

Ch. Von Storm's Emerson Prince Piet (Am. Can. Ch.
Nederlan Herman v. Mack ex Ch. Wallbridge's Best Bet),
wh. 1962. Breeder: Mrs. Nancy P. Riley. Owners: Mr. and
Mrs. Emerson P. Hempstead.

invitations were issued for her reception in the Sheraton Park Hotel to "meet" Ch. Clown. Seated on a velvet-covered table in the crowded banquet room, Clown held out his paw to greet government dignitaries and dog fanciers as they filed by. Needless to say, the affair drew considerable attention to the breed and made metropolitan newspaper headlines. In 1963, Mrs. McCormack presented to the Capital Kees Club a magnificent Specialty BOB Challenge Trophy in memory of her late husband, who had shared her interest in the Keeshonden in their Greenwich, Connecticut, home.

In 1954, Mr. Peterson and the author brought home from England Miss Hastings' 12-week-old Bacchus of Evenlode, and Mr. and Mrs. Fred Greenwood's Ch. Wot-A-Gal of Wistonia (in whelp to Eng. Ch. Wrocky of Wistonia). At ten-and-a-half months, Bacchus won the 1955 national Specialty from the classes, finished his championship in six straight shows, and placed in Groups the few times shown. Wot-A-Gal easily won her American title, and produced Am. Ch. Nederlan Winston of Wistonia.

In spite of the author's bumbling handling, Ch. Winston did quite well in his few shows with 35 BOB and four Firsts in 26 Group awards. Among his 11 champion offspring which figured in Groups, Mrs. Gertrude Clemmons' Ch. Theo v. Hergert (ex Nederlan Jilda v. Hansel) won the 1961 national Specialty, and Mrs. Norman Schaffer's Ch. Baron Mack of Keeshof (ex Nederlan Belinda v. Dirk) topped a Capital Keeshond Club show. But Winston's main role was as a progenitor of record-making Kees through line-breeding.

In 1959, Nederlan's owner-bred Ch. Nederlan Ursa v. Winston, a Winston daughter ex Ch. Erika of Waarheid, was bred to Mrs. Schaffer's Ch. Baron Mack. This mating combined pedigrees which included Eng. Am. and Can. Ch. Wrocky of Wistonia and his British background, and through Ch. Banner and others incorporated Ch. Wynstraat's Kerk and his Van Sandar and Evenlode ancestors. Two of the champions in this Ursa-Baron Mack litter were Am. and Can. Ch. Nederlan Herman v. Mack and Ch. Nederlan Bruno v. Mack, purchased as puppies by the Emerson P. Hempsteads of Greenwich, Connecticut, who became ardent exhibitors.

The Hempsteads rate vast credit for campaigning their pets. One result was that Ch. Herman topped all previous BIS, Group and Specialty records made by an American-bred Keeshond in Eastern competition. He took 10 BIS (two Canadian), 35 Group Firsts, 51

GR2, 26 GR3, and 11 GR4 in 143 BOB wins. He won eight Specialties: The Keeshond Club of America, The Capital Keeshond Club (4 times), and the huge entry Keeshond Club of Delaware Valley (3 times). Also, he is the sire of 11 champions.

Ch. Herman was in the Top Ten Non-Sporting in the Phillips System Ratings in 1964 (10th), 1965 (9th), and 1966 (9th). He won the Keeshond Club of America's trophies for the top-winning show dog owned by a member for four years.

In 1962, Herman and brother Bruno made a record sweep as Best Brace in Show at Westminster, Eastern Dog Club in Boston, and Chicago International. The Hempsteads again had a BIS brace in 1966 made up of Herman and a son, Ch. Von Storm's Emerson Prince Peit, bred by Mrs. Nancy Riley. Ch. Peit has thus far chalked up four BIS, 12 Groups, 13 GR2, and 18 other Group placings, won the 1966 and 1967 national Keeshond Club of America Specialties, and the 1967 Capital Keeshond Club Specialty.

Mrs. Virginia Ruttkay tells us that her Ruttkay Kennel got off to a slow start in Connecticut in 1946. Her foundation bitch, Brielle of Remlewood (by Conwood Roermond ex Azurka of Remlewood) was bought as a puppy from Jean Yock of Ohio, and is back of many Ruttkay Kees. Mrs. Ruttkay relates that Brielle was well-marked and "typey", and in spite of being small, finished her championship in 1951. In 1947, Brielle produced the first Ruttkay litter, all but one of which died from a virus despite supposed "immunization" by inoculations. Nero Van Beau, bred in California by Mrs. George Davis, sired Brielle's 1948 litter, and this included Ruttkay Skyrocket. Skyrocket sired three Ruttkay champions plus Ruttkay Romance, who became dam of Ch. Ruttkay Heir Apparent. Heir Apparent, owned and handled by Mrs. Pat Marcmann, recorded a 1958 Best in Show, six Groups and 27 other placings in his 50 Bests of Breed.

Other Ruttkay brood bitches were Conwood Gilda, obtained from Louis Todd's Kingleigh Kennel, Conwood Hildegard, bought from Mrs. Lillian O'Connor's Conwood Kennel in Canada (based mainly on British Vorden Kees), and Parkcliffe Mai van Pelt, bred by Gladys H. Jenkins. In 1952, Can. and Am. Ch. Conwood Kloos was purchased as a stud from the late Mr. Todd's granddaughter.

Mrs. Ruttkay's operation continued to increase its production and breeding stock after moving first to Virginia, and then to Pennsyl-

Ch. Ruttkay Roem (Ch. Van Ons Furious ex Ch. Ruttkay's Muuundawg), wh. 1958. Breeder-Owner: Ruttkay Kennels.

Irish Am. Ch. Karel of Altnavanog (Eng. Ch. Verschansing of Vorden ex Irish Ch. Kristine of Seafield), wh. 1950. Breeder: Doris M. Greene, Ireland. Owner: Ruttkay Kennels.

Ch. Ruttkay Heir Apparent (Ch. Karel of Altnavanog ex Ruttkay Romance), wh. 1955. Breeder: Ruttkay Kennel. Owner: Patricia Marcmann.

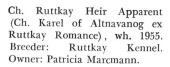

vania. Tenby Tina (by Eng. Ch. Lightning of Benthead ex Winmisty of Wistonia) was bought in the United States in 1953, as was Irish and Am. Ch. Karel of Altnavanog in 1955. Karel was by the distinguished Eng. Ch. Verschensing of Vorden ex Irish Ch. Kristine of Seafield. Among Karel's 12 champion get were Heir Apparent and Lorelei van Ruttkay. Lorelei, whose maternal great grandsire was Ch. Conwood Kloos, was the dam of five bench champions.

Ch. Ruttkay Roem (by Ch. Van Ons Furious ex Ch. Ruttkay Muundawg) was whelped in 1958, and became a notable stud. It is interesting that through his sire, bred by Mrs. Richard Koehne in Long Island, Roem was a grandson of Mrs. Vincent's Ch. Wynstraat's Kerk. Roem is the sire of 23 American champions (and one Canadian). Included in his offspring is Ch. Ruttkay Dutch Boy CD, owned and finished to both titles by Mrs. Earl Brandau of Milwaukee. Dutch Boy scored 12 Groups and many placings in the 1960s. Another Roem son was Ch. Ruttkay Moerdaag, who—as noted in our English chapter—was the first American-bred Keeshond exported to England (1963), where he won the *Razor Cup* as sire of the most winners in classes in a 1966 British specialty. Another first for Ruttkay was Cuban Ch. Ruttkay Achievement, who because there was no breed competition, gained his title by winning Groups. Due to conditions under the Castro regime, Achievement came back to the Ruttkay Kennel in 1960.

An addition to the Ruttkay stud force via Canada in 1966 was Can. Ch. Sinterklaas Brave Nimrod (by Eng. Ch. Big Bang of Evenlode ex Sinterklaas Lass of Vankeena), bred by Miss Collier in England. Nimrod gained an American title, and sired ten U.S. champions, as did Ruttkay's homebred Ch. Ruttkay Bold Venture. Also in the 1960's, Ch. Ruttkay Little Miss Napua (by Nederlan Brinker v. Winston ex Napua) was bred by Leo Calvacca, and went to Miss Linda Loucks in Minnesota, where she produced seven champions for Miss Loucks' Brynhaven Kennel.

In addition to widely advertising her kennel, Mrs. Ruttkay has used many different publicity media to promote the breed, such as articles and pictures in dog magazines, the *National Geographic* and its *Book of Dogs, Profitable Hobbies,* radio and television appearances, participation in Philadelphia's annual Dog Parade, etc. Her publicity program, together with the impressive number of 63 American champions bred by her (as owner or co-owner of bitches),

Ch. Ruttkay Bold Venture (Ch. Ruttkay's Chimney Sweep ex Ruttkay TV Star), wh. 1959. Breeder-owner: Ruttkay Kennels.

Can. Am. Ch. Sinterklaas Brave Nimrod (Eng. Ch. Big Bang of Evenlode ex Sinterklaas Lass of Vankeena), wh. 1962. Breeder: Mrs. Collier, England. Owner, Ruttkay Kennels.

Am. Can. Ch. Ruttkay Dutch Boy, CD (Ch. Ruttkay Roem ex Ruttkay Chimmy's Shady Lady), wh. 1961. Breeder: Virginia Ruttkay. Owners: Mr. and Mrs. Earl E. Brandau.

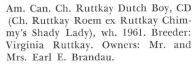

101

Ch. Van Fitz Hocage (Eng. Am. Ch. Tom Tit of Evenlode ex Moisje van Fitz), wh. 1950. Dam of 8 champions. Breeder: Vera Fitzpatrick. Owner, Dirdon Kennels.

Ch. Lorelei van Ruttkay (Ch. Karel of Altnavanog ex Ruttkay Secret), wh. 1956. Dam of 5 champions. Breeder-owner: Ruttkay Kennels.

Ch. Ruttkay Zilver Frost van Roem (Ch. Ruttkay Roem ex Empress Cleopatra), wh. 1962. Dam of 7 champions. Breeder: Virginia Ruttkay. Owner: Dolores M. Scharff.

have undoubtedly added greatly to public awareness of the breed. Mrs. Ruttkay was a charter member of the Keeshond Club of Delaware Valley, founded in 1961, and has served as a vice-president.

Mrs. E. J. Cummings II had been active in Obedience training and raising Cockers for several years before her son acquired Wynstraat's Cover Boy in 1950. But this Kees puppy led to Mr. and Mrs. Cummings' establishment of their Dirdon Kennel in Long Island to breed and exhibit Keeshonden as a hobby. While their son was in service in the Korean war, Mrs. Cummings trained and handled Cover Boy from his CDX to UD, and took part in many of the Keeshond Club's Obedience Team's successful competitions with other breeds' teams, and in exhibitions they gave for charitable organizations.

Mrs. Cummings' Van Fitz Hocage (by Ch. Tom Tit of Evenlode ex Moisje Van Fitz), from Mrs. Fitzpatrick's Van Fitz kennel in California, proved to be a splendid brood bitch. In three litters sired by Ch. Wynstraat's Kerk, Ch. Hocage produced eight champions, the most notable of which was Ch. Dirdon's Durk Donder. Mrs. Cummings' extensive campaigning of Durk Donder as breeder-owner and amateur handler was an important contribution to bringing the breed to public attention at the shows. An impressive, super-coated dog, Durk Donder's presentation and showmanship won him quite a record in the late 1950's. He not only followed his sire, Kerk, as the second Keeshond to go Best in Show in the East, but won 3 BIS, 14 Groups and 42 placings in 70 Bests of Breed, including BOB at the 1956 and 1957 national Specialty shows. Moreover, he sired the BIS winner, Ch. Wynstraat's Garry, CD.

Two of Durk Donder's brothers also put Kees in the spotlight. In 1956, Ch. Dirdon's Helder Zwier CD and Ch. Dirdon's Wonder Wander Hocage CD, owned, trained, and amateur-handled by Mrs. Marye Picone of Long Island, became the first Keeshond brace to take Best Brace in Show at Westminster, and also topped the braces at the big Albany show that year. Mrs. Picone's activities in the breed included her work as secretary, and later treasurer, of the Keeshond Club of America.

After Fred Dohrmann's homebred Ch. Hanzel van Dohrmann (a grandson of Ch. Tom Tit of Evenlode) was added to Dirdon Kennel, he completed his CDX, and won the 1960 Keeshond Club of America Specialty. Bred to Dirdon's Ch. Dirdon's Fancy, CD, Hanzel sired Ch. Dirdon's Fancy Dan and seven other champion get. Though shown

103

only rarely after finishing, Fancy Dan won some big Groups in the 1960s.

Mr. Cummings II was president of the Keeshond Club of America for six years until he withdrew from that office in 1962, and became the club's treasurer and delegate to the American Kennel Club. Mrs. Cummings served four years as the national club's secretary, during which time she also wrote the KCA's Keeshond column in the AKC's *Purebred Dogs—American Kennel Gazette.* As an AKC-approved Obedience and Keeshond judge, Mrs. Cummings' many assignments have included judging the breed in the Specialties of the Capital Keeshond Club in 1962, and the Keeshond Club of America in 1963.

Mrs. Lois McNamara's purchase of a puppy bitch named Sweetie Pie from Mrs. Ethel Miller in 1954 was the reason Wil-Los Kennel and the Capital Keeshond Club came into existence in the Washington D.C. area. Mrs. McNamara's kennel had its start in 1956, when Sweetie Pie (by Ch. Nether-Lair's Banner de Gyselaer ex Mrs. Miller's Ch. Ruttkay Dutch Treat) was bred to Nederlan Kennel's Ch. Bacchus of Evenlode, and produced Ch. Heineken CD. Heineken was sold as a puppy to Mr. and Mrs. James MacMartin, who—with Mrs. McNamara as secretary, and Mr. MacMartin as president— founded the Capital Keeshond Club in 1957.

Mrs. McNamara's rescue of an apparently unwanted and mistreated Keeshond was a shining example of what understanding, humane treatment can do to help unfortunate dogs. Mrs. McNamara found D'el Dee Dunkel Ferbig Duke (by Ch. Conwood Kloos ex Pegel Recall) on a so-called "dog farm", where he had been dumped by previous owners. He was a terrified animal, suspicious of everyone. Months of Mrs. McNamara's gentle care and training in her home restored Duke's confidence in people, and brought out his inherent characteristics as a happy, affectionate pet. As a result, he became a champion, completed the CD degree, and sired three title winners for Wil-Los Kennel.

Among this kennel's many champions, Ch. Wil-Los Jamie Boy (by Wil-Los Big Surprise Wilhelm ex Mrs. Eleanore Knapp's Knappholme's Kool Kolors) played a leading role as a stud and show dog. Owner-handled, he took four Groups plus 15 other placings, was the first Keeshond to win the Westchester KC's Group, won a Capital Club Specialty, and won the inaugural Keeshond Club of Delaware Valley Specialty in 1962, over what was then a record entry for the

Ch. Dirdon's Durk Donder (Ch. Wynstraat's Kerk ex Ch. Van Fitz Hocage), wh. 1952. Breeder-owner: Mrs. E. J. Cummings II, Dirdon Kennels.

Ch. Wil-Los Jamie Boy (Wil-Los Big Surprise Wilhelm ex Knappholme's Kool Kolors), wh. 1958. Breeder: Mrs. Eleanor Knapp. Owner: Mrs. Lois S. McNamara.

Ch. Van Ons Gladly (Ch. Van Fitz Bingo ex Ch. Van Ons Balda). Breeder: Van Ons Kennels (Mrs. Richard Koehne). Owner: Mrs. George Jones, Alaska.

105

breed in the United States of 99 dogs. In 1964, Jamie Boy won the Keeshond Club of America's Trophy for Best Member-Owned Stud as sire of the most champions finished that year. It is his head that is depicted on the Capital Club's seal and membership pin. Included in the 14 champions he sired was the top-flight show dog, Ch. Mar-I-Ben Licorice Twist (ex Ch. Wil-Los Zoet Zang), bred and owned by Miss Marilyn Bender.

In 1967 the Capital Keeshond Club presented commemorative plaques to Mr. and Mrs. McNamara, and to Mr. and Mrs. Mac-Martin, in recognition of their founding of the club, and their contributions to its success.

Mrs. Richard Koehne's Van Ons Kennel in Long Island, New York, bred 11 champions of merit. Ch. Van Ons Gladly (by Ch. Van Fitz Bingo ex Ch. Van Ons Balda) went to Mrs. George Jones in Alaska, where he was the first Keeshond to take Best in Show and Groups in that area. Mrs. Koehne's imported Ch. Amanda of Evenlode was distinguished by whelping five American title winners. The four in one litter by Ch. Wynstraat's Kerk were Chs. Van Ons Fussy Hussy, Furious, Frantic, and Firecracker, and Ch. Van Ons Ipso Facto's father was Ch. Kenmerk Hallmark. Van Ons Furious sired Ch. Ruttkay Roem, and Firecracker produced five champions bred by her owners, the E. J. Cummings III.

Ch. Fussy Hussy was a foundation bitch for Mrs. Gwen Worley's successful Kenmerk Kennel in Amarillo, Texas, and contributed five of Kenmerk's 13 champions sired by the imported Am. Ch. Emissory of Evenlode. One of the five was Ch. Kenmerk Heiress, the dam of Ch. Wallbridge's Best Bet, a famous bitch ring star bred by Mrs. Douglas Wallbridge of Schenectady, New York. Another was Ch. Kenmerk Hallmark, who won the 1962 national Specialty and an all-breed Best in Show, owner-handled by Mrs. R. B. Hollaman of Darien, Connecticut.

Mrs. Hollaman's homebred Ch. Van Geest Doorn (by Eng. and Am. Ch. Vaalsmeer of Vorden ex. Ch. Van Ons Ipso Facto) was the first Bermudian Keeshond champion, a title acquired by Group wins. In addition to Mrs. Hollaman's activities in breed and Obedience, her work as secretary of The Keeshond Club of America from 1962 through many years, has been an invaluable asset to the organization.

The ring successes of Mr. and Mrs. Earl Brandau with their Am. and Can. Ch. Ruttkay Dutch Boy CD (by Ch. Ruttkay Roem ex

Ch. Kenmerk Hallmark (Ch. Emmissory of Evenlode ex Ch. Van Ons Fussy Hussy), wh. 1959. Breeder: Gwen Worley. Owners: Van Ons Kennels and Mrs. Richard B. Hollaman.

Ch. Emissory of Evenlode (Dutch-Downlander of Evenlode ex Evenlode Anuke of Goss), wh. 1957. Breeder: Miss O. M. Hastings, England. Owner: Gwen Worley.

Ch. Van Ons Fussy Hussy (Ch. Wynstraat's Kerk ex Ch. Amanda of Evenlode), wh. 1955. Dam of 5 champions. Breeder: Van Ons Kennels. Owner: Gwen Worley.

107

Ruttkay Chimmy's Shady Lady) were an auspicious start for their Wind Mill Kennel in Milwaukee. Dutch Boy collected 12 Group blues and many placements, and was also a Canadian Group winner. His sire, Ch. Ruttkay Roem, was by Ch. Van Ons Furious, and Dutch Boy's maternal grandsire was Ch. Ruttkay Chimney Sweep, who sired eight champions.

Mr. and Mrs. John A. Lafore, Jr. were prominent Collie breeders from 1948 until they bought their first Keeshond in 1955, a puppy bitch who they called "Puff Ball", but whose official name was Ruttkay Secret Love. An appropriate name for a new member of a Collie household. From then on, the Lafores were devotees of Keeshonden, and in comparatively few years their Chantwood Kennel in Haverford, Pennsylvania was the home of 18 champions that had enjoyed impressive successes in the Group.

The records show that British Vorden Kees played a predominant part in Chantwood's successul breeding program. The kennel's breeding stock, composed of Ch. Ruttkay Secret Love, Ch. Ruttkay Silver Spray, imported Virginia of Vorden, and Am. Ch. Voljester of Vorden, all had a common ancestor in Eng. Ch. Verschansing of Vorden. Am. Ch. Virginia of Vorden (by Eng. Ch. Young Geron of Evenlode ex Eng. Ch. Veraura of Vorden) distinguished herself as the dam of six Chantwood title-winners.

Under the leadership of Mr. Lafore as president, and Mrs. Lafore as secretary, the Keeshond Club of Delaware Valley was organized in 1958. Less than two years later, the Club held the first of its record-breaking Specialty shows, one of which is believed to be a world record for Keeshond entries. Among the first of Mrs. Lafore's assignments as an AKC-approved Keeshond judge was the judging of the Keeshond Club of Southern California 1967 Specialty at Beverly Hills.

Mr. Lafore has been an eminent member of the Board of Directors of the Keeshond Club of America and of the American Kennel Club. In 1968, he became Executive Vice-President of the AKC, an honor that benefited dogdom at the expense of Keeshond interest. Unfortunately, American Kennel Club policy does not permit officials or their families to show dogs or judge. Not long before Mr. Lafore took on the AKC post, Chantwood had imported Waakzaam Wollenhoven from Mrs. E. M. Smyth in England. Wollenhoven made his

Ch. Virginia of Vorden (Eng. Ch. Young Geron of Evonlode ex Ch. Veraura of Vorden), wh. 1956. Dam of 6 champions. Breeder: Mrs. I. M. Tucker, England. Owners: Margaret R. and John A. Lafore, Jr.

Ch. Waakzaam Wollenhoven (Waakzaam Woten ex Waakzaam Wonderbarlijk), wh. 1966. Breeder: Mrs. E. M. Smyth, England. Owners: Mr. and Mrs. John A. Lafore, Jr. (later transferred to Mr. and Mrs. Stuart Duncan).

Ch. Rhapsody of Westcrest (Eng. Am. Ch. Wylco of Wistonia ex Ch. Ruttkay Winsome), wh. 1961. Bitch Group winner and dam of 6 champions. Breeder: Jane V. West. Owner: Marguerite K. Goebel.

American debut by winning two Groups from the classes. He was later acquired by Mr. and Mrs. Stuart Duncan, and in limited showing has—at time of this writing—scored a total of 6 Group Firsts, 5 Seconds, and 8 other placements.

The first litter for Mrs. Ellen Stoodley's Coventry Forge Kennel in Pennsylvania was bred in 1956, and was by Knappholme's Kolijet ex Ch. Knappholme's Kirza. The kennel is one of the few in the United States which have owned Dutch-bred Kees. In fact, its first homebred champion was Ch. Coventry's Frederick CD, and was sired by the Dutch import Sigelinski's Quality ex Verber Vaskti. More Dutch dogs were subsequently procured, including Belgian and German Ch. Sigelinski's Brijitte. With several Wistonia Kees from England, they formed the basis of Coventry Forge's breeding program, which became a sizeable operation.

More than 20 champions and eight Obedience titlists have been bred, owned or produced by the kennel. The consistent success of Coventry puppies in Eastern Specialty shows has been especially notable. In 1967, the record was highlighted by Mrs. Stoodley's win of the Keeshond Club of America's Puppy Futurity Stake with her 8-months-old Coventry's Thunderstruck, by Mrs. Phyllis Noonan's Ch. Robs Macduff of Sherwood ex Coventry's Torrid Weather. Later that year, Mrs. Stoodley was married to Mr. Alfred J. Horrox. Futurity and Best of Opposite Sex, both by the Horrox's Kennel. The 1968 Best in Futurity and Best of Opposite Sex winners were both bred by the Horrox's Kennel.

I appreciate Mrs. Stoodley having typed, for my use, copies of the American Kennel Club Stud Book's Keeshond registration records from 1930 through 1945. This kindness saved me from spending that many more hours of research in the AKC's library in New York.

Mrs. Ronald West of Bunker Hill, West Virginia, was a founder and secretary, and subsequently president of the Capital Keeshond Club, and in the 1960s joined the Board of Directors of the Keeshond Club of America. Her Westcrest Kennel champions included homebred Rhapsody of Westcrest, who was a result of line-breeding of Kees whose own and their antecedents' attributes had won recognition in American and English show rings, and who had themselves in turn produced winners. Rhapsody was by Flakkee Kennel's imported Eng. and Am. Ch. Wylco of Wistonia, and out of Mrs. West's

110

Ch. Ruttkay Winsome, a daughter of Ch. Nederlan Winston of Wistonia ex Ch. Lorelei v. Ruttkay.

Acquired as a puppy by Mrs. Max Goebel, Rhapsody was a foundation bitch for her successful Fairville Kennel in Chadds Ford, Pennsylvania. Rhapsody was off to a fast start, at age of only 9 months winning BOS at the Capital Keeshond Club's 1962 Specialty. Her Group victory the next month, handled by her amateur-owner from the classes, made her the second Keeshond bitch to win an Eastern Group, and undoubtedly the youngest. Ch. Rhapsody's influence on the breed as a brood bitch was even more noteworthy. In her three litters, sired respectively by Eng. Am. and Can. Ch. Wrocky of Wistonia, Eng. and Am. Ch. Whiplash of Wistonia, and Am. and Can. Ch. Nederlan Herman v. Mack, she produced six of Fairville's eight homebred champions.

The results of the 1966 Keeshond Club of America's Futurity were a breeder's dream come true for Mrs. Goebel. Her Fairville puppies, by Ch. Whiplash ex Ch. Rhapsody, took Best in Futurity, and Best of Opposite Sex. Mrs. Goebel was the breeder, too, of Mrs. West's Intermezzo of Fairville, who took Best Opposite to the Best in Futurity in 1967. Mrs. Goebel was a charter member of The Keeshond Club of Delaware Valley, a director and its treasurer, and in 1969 took on assignment as treasurer of the Keeshond Club of America.

Mrs. Nancy Riley, a former German Shepherd Dog fancier, became enthused over the charms of the Keeshonden when in 1959 she obtained Mrs. Cowley's Nether-Lair's Vali de Gyselaer and Ch. Nether-Lair's Bard de Gyselaer CD. In a very few years, her Von Storm Kennel in Millport, New York achieved outstanding success.

Ch. Bard placed in quite a few Groups, but his main importance was that two of his get became the top-winning Keeshond bitches in the country in 1963, 1964, and 1965 (based on points for their Group wins and placings). These famous females were litter sisters out of Ch. Kenmerk Heiress who had been purchased by Mrs. Douglas Wallbridge from Mrs. Worley in Texas. Mr. and Mrs. H. Philip Shoudy bought and showed Ch. Wallbridge's Valasko Smokey to her triumphs as the 1963 and 1964 winner, and the 1965 star was Mrs. Riley's Ch. Wallbridge's Best Bet.

In two litters, Ch. Best Bet produced ten of Von Storm's 15 distinguished champions. Among the five sired by Ch. Nederlan Herman v. Mack, the Hempsteads' Ch. Von Storm's Emerson Prince Piet was a BIS, Group and Speciality winner of note. Mrs. Riley's Ch. Von Storm's Emaria was the 1966 top Keeshond show bitch in the United States. And Ch. Von Storm's Electra became in turn, the dam of six champions in a litter bred by Rodney Nickerson. Best Bet's second litter was by the Carl I. Gettigs' great stud, Ch. Vereeren of Vorden, and contributed four more titlists. Her tenth champion was by Mr. Al Hull's Ch. Roblin's Gift to Stoney Hill. It was a big loss to the breed when in 1967 Mrs. Riley found it necessary to give up raising Kees, but since 1968 she has been active as an AKC-approved judge.

Another owner who has had success as a breeder in a short time has been Miss Linda Loucks in Minnesota. Her Ch. Ruttkay Little Miss Napua (by Nederlan Hans Brinker ex Napua) whelped six Brynhaven champions for Miss Loucks, and two of Little Miss Napua's puppies (by Ch. Ruttkay Bold Adventure) took Best Brace in Show at 1966 Minnesota and Wisconsin shows.

Before Mr. and Mrs. Roger Van Houten of Elmhurst, New York had ever seen a dog show or a Keeshond, they spent their leisure hours on their cabin cruiser, accompanied by Rex, a much-loved, beautiful mongrel. After Rex died, they bought a Keeshond puppy registered as Koning van de Duizelen, which in Dutch means "King of the Devils". But Koning, or "Little Rex" as they called him, was the absolute opposite of a devil, and starting in 1959, soon made the Van Houtens forget their boat and devote all their spare time to the show rings, breeding Kees, and Obedience training.

They obtained Wynfomeer's Firedancer as a foundation bitch, finished her and Koning, and in remarkably few years, the Van Houtens' Rovic Kennel had produced five owner-bred-handled-and-trained breed champions, with a total among them of five CD's, two CDX's, and one UD, along with four placements in the Group. Rovic's most spectacular dual title winner was Ch. Rovic's Chimney Blaze, UD (by Mrs. McNamara's Ch. Ruttkay Chimney Sweep ex Ch. Wynfomeer's Firedancer, CDX). The record of Ch. Blaze's great career as a star Obedience performer will be found in the chapter on The Keeshond in Obedience.

Mrs. Van Houten has for several years been the Keeshond Club of America's National Obedience Recording Chairman.

Mr. and Mrs. Carl I. Gettig of Pleasant Gap, Pennsylvania, looked into the characteristics of many breeds as pets and decided that the Keeshond was the dog for them. In 1962, after having enjoyed the

Ch. Wallbridge's Best Bet (Ch. Nether-Lair's Bard de Gyselaer, CD ex Ch. Kenmerk Heiress), wh. 1961. Dam of 10 champions and the top winning Keeshond bitch in the United States for 1966. Breeder: Betty Lou Wallbridge. Owner: Nancy P. Riley.

Ch. Vereeren of Vorden (Eng. Ch. Big Bang of Evenlode ex Verkorten of Vorden), wh. 1962. Breeder: Mrs. Irene M. Tucker, England. Owners: Mr. and Mrs. Carl I. Gettig.

Von Storm's Electra (Ch. Nederlan Herman v. Mack ex Ch. Wallbridge's Best Bet), wh. 1962. Dam of 6 champions. Breeder: Nancy P. Riley. Owner: Rodney Nickerson.

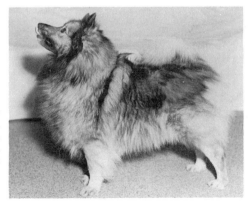

113

companionship of Ruttkay Hallmark for nine years, they obtained young Vereeren of Vorden (by Eng. Ch. Big Bang of Evenlode ex Verkorten of Vorden) from Mrs. Irene Tucker's British kennel. Vereeren's second showing brought him the Reserve Winners Dog ribbon in the 1962 Keeshond Club of Delaware Valley's first record-breaking Specialty. Shown but moderately, "Jon"—as Vereeren was called at home—achieved quite a record, winning the 1963, 1964 and 1968 national Specialties of the Keeshond Club of America (all under breeder judges), and in 1968 went on to win Best in Show at Trenton on the same day, scoring over 3,180 dogs, the largest entry ever topped by a Keeshond in the United States.

The marked resemblance of his 11 champion get and 6 Obedience titlists to their sire has shown that Vereeren had the important and somewhat rare ability to transmit his own excellent attributes to his puppies, who in turn passed them on to their progeny. At six successive national Specialties, Ch. Vereeren was judged Best Stud, based on the quality of two of his get in each show, and he won the Keeshond Club of America's Stud Trophy at the member-owned sire of the most champions finished in 1968.

Mrs. Gettig was the Keeshond Club of America's official Keeshond columnist in the *Pure Bred Dogs—American Kennel Gazette* for the five years before 1968. She was also appointed the club representative to The Orthopedic Foundation for Animals in that year. In 1969 Mr. Gettig became the club president.

Ch. Ruttkay Zilver Frost van Roem (by Ch. Ruttkay Roem ex Empress Cleopatra), bred by Virginia Ruttkay and whelped in 1962, became the property of Mrs. Dolores Scharff. "Fabulous Frosty", as she was called by her owner, did well in the breed rings under Mrs. Scharff's professional handling, and made quite a name for herself as the dam of six champions of merit.

Miss Marilyn Bender was in her twenties when her Mar-I-Ben Kennel in North Canton, Ohio first became famous. Her homebred Ch. Mar-I-Ben Licorice Twist, co-owned and amateur-handled by her friend, Mrs. Robert Geiger, won two BIS, 14 Groups, and 62 other Group ribbons in the 1960's. What's more, Licorice Twist's dam, Ch. Wil-Los Zoet Zang (by Ch. Ruttkay Chimney Sweep ex Wil-Los Lady Roxanne), who was bred by Mrs. Lois McNamara, became a star in her own right. In each of Zoet Zang's two litters by Ch. Wil-Los Jamie Boy, she produced five Mar-I-Ben champions. An

114

Ch. Mar-I-Ben Licorice Twist (Ch. Wil-Los Jamie Boy ex Ch. Wil-Los Zoet Zang), wh. 1962. Breeder: Marilyn B. Bender. Owners: Marilyn B. Bender and Eloise W. Geiger.

Ch. Wil-Los Zoet Zang (Ch. Ruttkay's Chimney Sweep ex Wil-Los Lady Roxanne), wh. 1960. Dam of 10 champions. Breeders: Lois S. and Wm. C. McNamara. Owner: Marilyn B. Bender.

Best in Show Brace, Ch. Mar-I-Ben Singapore Sling, and sire, Ch. Mar-I-Ben Licorice Twist. Breeder: Marilyn B. Bender. Owners: Marilyn B. Bender and Eloise W. Geiger.

115

outstanding record, augmented by the fact that many of these ten champions did exceedingly well in Group competition.

Miss Bender received many honors in connection with her service and success in the breed. The Capital Keeshond Club's *Kultz Challenge Trophy* for the top-winning, member-owned show dog was retired in 1966 by Ch. Licorice Twist, as a three-time winner. In 1963, Miss Bender's name was the first inscribed upon the Keeshond Club of America's Kultz Challenge Trophy for the national club's member-breeder of the most champions finished within the year.

When the Lakeshore Keeshond Club was first formed in Ohio, with Mrs. Clinton Carlton as president, Miss Bender and Mrs. Geiger were charter members. They became president and secretary respectively, and when, after Miss Bender's illness, the club became known as the Buckeye Keeshond Club, they continued as members of the Board of Directors. In 1969, Mrs. Geiger judged the Keeshond Club of America's Puppy Futurity Stake.

The immediate success of young Rodney Nickerson of Jamestown, N.Y. with his first Keenic Kennel litter was phenomenal. His achievements were clearly based on a studious approach to breeding dogs, and were interrelated with the attainments of Miss Bender, Mrs. Nancy Riley, and others.

While Rodney was still a high school student, he decided to find a suitable young Keeshond bitch for breeding and show. From several possibilities suggested by Mrs. E. J. Cummings II, to whom he had written for advice, he chose Mrs. Riley's Von Storm's Electra, who was by Ch. Nederlan Herman v. Mack ex Ch. Wallbridge's Best Bet. He showed Electra to her championship, and bred her to Miss Bender's Ch. Mar-I-Ben Licorice Twist, which mating produced six Keenic champions.

One of the puppies in the litter was Keenic's Turf Commander. Rodney was barely nineteen when, in 1965, he and Turf Commander won the KCA's First Puppy Futurity, judged by Mrs. Gladys Baldwin. Then, under a different judge, Turf Commander took Best of Winners in the club's regular Specialty classes.

Rodney's subsequent win of a leg on the national club's Kultz Breeder's Challenge Trophy (for "Breeder of the Year") in 1965, made him not only the youngest to have won the honor, but the only one to have won it with a first litter.

The next Keenic litter was by Ch. Keenic's Guided Missile ex Ch. Von Storm's Helena, and was also a standout. One of the puppies

116

had finished, and several others were well on their way to championship, before their breeder was called for military service.

A 1967 issue of *Kee Topics* magazine, edited by Mr. and Mrs. W. D. Westcott, for the Keeshond Club of Delaware Valley, cited Mr. Nickerson's reply to a request for his suggestions for novice breeders. The ideas he expressed merit consideration by *all* breeders. He listed:

1. Patience and deep study in selecting a bitch.
2. Seek help from knowledgeable breeders and exhibitors.
3. Keep a list of the faults prevalent in each of your dogs and their ancestors, going back at least to the second generation, and in litters from them, if possible. Prejudice or "kennel blindness" may limit the success of this. An easy way to check on whether you are kennel blind is to see whether your dogs have as many, or more faults, than others. You should evaluate your own dogs thoroughly. Being extremely critical keeps you from being too self-satisfied.

Ch. Vonfossens Isis (Ch. Sinterklaas Brave Nimrod ex Ch. Clareton Tami), wh. 1966. Bitch Group winner. Breeder: Ivan Reaves. Owners: Patricia and Ralph Martinez.

The West Coast

We now turn to California where Kees and their owners have made spectacular national records, and the dogs' wins established historical firsts for the breed in America.

The Keeshond was introduced on the West Coast in 1932 when Irving Florsheim sent a puppy bitch to Mrs. Kenneth Fitzpatrick in Encino, California, which she registered as Guelder Fitzpatrick. Mrs. Fitzpatrick then started the Van Fitz Kennel, and her lifelong interest in Kees was greatly responsible for the extensive and continuing activities of breeders and exhibitors in that area.

In 1934, Tilly Van Fitz of Canford and a young male, Dynasty of Canford, a son of Eng. Ch. Bingo, were purchased from Mrs. E. Harrison of Canford, England. In 1936, Dynasty was the first male Keeshond Group winner. He won eight Groups, placed 10 times, and made more breed history in 1939 as the first Keeshond in America to win an all-breed Best in Show. For eleven years, Dynasty was undefeated in the breed, and in 1937 one of his sons, Ch. Dirk Van Fitz, was the first Keeshond to earn a CD title on the West Coast.

Guelder Wiegbold (by Guelder Flock ex Guelder Aria), a heavy-coated, very light gray dog bred by Mrs. Gatacre in England, was imported by Mrs. Fitzpatrick as a stud to lighten color in the 1940's, and became a Group and Best in Show winner in the United States.

Patriot Van Fitz, by Mr. Mancel Clark's Clovelly Kris ex Ch. Kenise Van Fitz, was a Van Fitz homebred that made breed history. Patriot was sold as a puppy to Mrs. Van Cott Niven (later, Mrs. Porter Washington), the founder of Flakkee Kennel, and in 1948 he became the first American-bred Best in Show winner.

The next Van Fitz import was Eng. Ch. Tom Tit of Evenlode. He was a great stud and show dog who sired 17 American champions including a BIS dog and Group winners. In his 20 shows in the United States, Tom Tit won 3 BIS, 10 Groups, and many placements. While Tom Tit was making this record, Mrs. Fitzpatrick's homebred Ch. Taes II Van Fitz chalked up a Best in Show, 15 Group wins, and 32 Group placements. On the same day that Tom Tit took BIS in Texas, handled by his owner, her Ch. Taes won the Group in Pennsylvania, and her imported Can. and Am. Ch. Conwood Mia placed in the Group in California. Quite a record for one owner on one day!

Ch. Dynasty of Canford, wh.
1934, the first Keeshond to win
Best in Show in the United
States (1939). By Eng. Ch. Bingo
ex Duskie Dinah, Dynasty was
bred by Mrs. E. Harrison, England, and owned by Vera and
Kenneth Fitzpatrick.

Ch. Guelder Wiegbold (Guelder
Flock ex Guelder Aria), wh.
1938. Breeder: Mrs. W. E. Gatacre, England. Owners: Vera and
Kenneth Fitzpatrick.

Ch. Taes II Van Fitz (Conwood
Kurt, Can. import ex Trienje
van Fitz), wh. 1948. Breederowners: Vera and Kenneth Fitzpatrick.

Mrs. Fitzpatrick's handsome Ch. Van Fitz Bingo, who was by Ch. Tom Tit of Evenlode ex William Teeter's Dulcie Van Fitz, was outstanding as an American-bred winner of 6 Bests in Show and 22 Groups in the 1950s. After judging at the Cheltenham show in England, Mrs. Fitzpatrick brought home Am. Ch. Vandina of Vanellen, who produced five American champions. Moisje Van Fitz was the dam of eight title winners.

The Van Fitz records of BIS Brace and Team wins at the two biggest shows in California will not often be equalled by one exhibitor. For three straight years, starting in 1938, Ch. Dynasty of Canford and Ch. Dirk Van Fitz took Best Brace in Show, and with Chs. Geraad Van Gaardha and Dennis Van Fitz were members of BIS Teams. In 1942, Ch. Dynasty and Ch. Dirk again took top Brace honors. Ch. Gungadin Van Fitz with Ch. Clovelly Van Fitz were a 1946 BIS Brace, and in 1952 and 1954, Ch. Tom Tit and his son, Ch. Van Fitz Bingo, brought two more BIS Brace rosettes to the Van Fitz Kennel.

Under Mrs. Fitzpatrick's leadership as president, the Pacific Coast Keeshond Club, later named the Keeshond Club of Southern California, was formed in 1940. Mrs. Fitzpatrick judged the 1950 Keeshond Club of America Specialty at Long Island, New York, and was the national club's president in 1955. Her tragic death that year was a great loss to the breed to which she had brought so much recognition, through her important imports and the extensive showing of her record-making Keeshonden.

In 1957, Mr. Fitzpatrick added another great import to the Van Fitz record. This was Mrs. Irene Tucker's Vangabang of Vorden, whose famous dam was Eng. Ch. Volkrijk of Vorden, the 1957 Best in Show winner at Crufts in England over 6,562 entries. Vangabang became a top-ranking winner in the United States in his own right with 5 BIS, 45 Group Firsts, 66 GR2, and 39 other Group placings. He also brought national attention to the breed as the first Keeshond to figure in the Phillips System Ratings, started in 1956, placing sixth highest of all Non-Sporting dogs in the United States for 1958, and seventh for 1959. Also in 1958, Vangabang became the first Keeshond to receive the Quaker Oats Award, winning more Group Firsts than any other dog of any breed in the Far West division of the country.

One of Am. Ch. Vangabang's eight champion get was Mr. and Mrs.

Eng. Am. Ch. Tom Tit of Evenlode (Vandyke of Vorden ex Lucinda of Evenlode), wh. 1946. Breeder: Miss O. M. Hastings, England. Owners: Mr. and Mrs. Kenneth Fitzpatrick.

Ch. Vangabang of Vorden (Eng. Ch. Big Bang of Evenlode ex Eng. Ch. Volkrijk of Vorden), wh. 1956. Breeder: Mrs. I. M. Tucker, England. Owner: Kenneth Fitzpatrick.

Charles Mulock's Ch. Rikki van Armel CD (ex Ch. Wilhelmina of Kittridge), bred by Walter Winkler. Handled by Mr. Mulock, Ch. Rikki became the first dual title-holding Keeshond to go Best in Show.

Ch. Klaas of Kittridge (by Ch. Armel Jeremias ex Mil-Em Majorette), bred by Norman Coci, was also purchased by Mr. Fitzpatrick. Klaas added eight more Group blues and 41 placements for Van Fitz–owned dogs, and won four Keeshond Club of Southern California Specialties.

The Walter Dayringers' homebred Ch. Jul-Day Snoodark, a son of Ch. Vangabang ex Ch. Jul-Day Wunderlust de Sylvia UD, was obtained by Mr. Fitzpatrick in 1967 and carried on as another highly successful Van Fitz winner. In just one year in the rings as a champion, Snoodark took 2 BIS, 12 Group Firsts, 12 GR2, and 8 other placings before his untimely death.

The breed owes much to Mr. and Mrs. Fitzpatrick for the roles they have played in the progress of the Keeshond in America.

Among the many fine Kees produced by Mancel Clark, Jr.'s Clovelly Kennel in California in the late 1930's, Ch. Beau Van Fitz of Clovelly (by the Florsheims' Bright Clouds Over Red Top ex Veda Van Fitz of Clovelly) was purchased by the George Davises. The Davises were among the founders of the Pacific Coast Keeshond Club, with Mr. Davis as its first secretary, and later, president. Mrs. Davis has continued as the club's historian, and we are indebted to her for the information about the club and some of the California fanciers.

Mr. Clark became an AKC-approved judge and presided over the Keeshond Club of Delaware Valley's big 1964 Specialty in Pennsylvania.

Kees broke into the movies when, in 1942, Mr. Davis' Non-Sporting Group Brace winners, Ch. Beau Beau Van Fitz of Clovelly and a son, Fidel van Beau of Ivar, appeared in a widely distributed Paramount picture entitled *A Day at a Dog Show*. And Mrs. Fitzpatrick's Ch. Dirk Van Fitz CD was in a film with Simone Simone.

Other southern Californians who became successful breeders and exhibitors were Miss Grace Radford, Mr. and Mrs. James A. Grant, Jr., Mrs. Rose Hale, Miss Melba Jones, Mr. and Mrs. Walter Winkler, Mrs. Helen Geist, Mr. and Mrs. Robert Blachnik, and Mr. Wendell Pratt. Many of them were also officials of the Southern Cali-

Ch. Rikki van Armel, CD—the first dual-titled Keeshond to win Best in Show in the United States (1961). (Ch. Vangabang of Vorden ex Ch. Wilhelmina of Kittridge.) Breeder: Walter Winkler. Owners: Mr. and Mrs. Charles M. Mulock.

Ch. Vandina of Vanellin (Colin of Ossen ex Wilki of Wistonia), wh. 1950 in England. Dam of 5 American champions. Owners: Vera and Kenneth Fitzpatrick.

Ch. Van Fitz Bingo (Eng. Am. Ch. Tom Tit of Evenlode ex Dulcie van Fitz), wh. 1950. Breeder: Tom Teeter. Owners: Vera and Kenneth Fitzpatrick.

Ch. Jul-Day Snoodark (Ch. Vangabang of Vorden ex Ch. Jul-Day Wunderlust de Sylvia, UD), wh. 1963. Breeders: Julia and Walter Dayringer. Owner: Kenneth Fitzpatrick.

123

fornia club. Miss Jones judged record entries at the 1963 Keeshond Club of Delaware Valley Specialty, and at the Keeshond Club of America's national event in 1969.

Few names, if any, may ever hold a more eminent position in the Keeshond's show history in America than Flakkee Kennel, and its owners, Mr. and Mrs. Porter Washington of Beverly Hills, California. Some years before Mrs. Van Cott Niven became Mrs. Washington, she was captivated by 8-weeks-old Dutch Van Hogan. In 1939, she bought Dutch, and then Punch Van Fitz and later Patriot Van Fitz from Mrs. Fitzpatrick, and fortunately for the breed, started Flakkee Kennel.

Patriot was the first in the long list of illustrious show stars that Flakkee was to exhibit to top rank among the nation's Best in Show and Group winners, all handled throughout their careers by Mr. Washington, and year after year bringing increased renown to the breed.

Patriot became the first American-bred Best in Show winner. In 1948, he sired Flakkee's first homebred champion, Flakkee Dusky Devil, whose dam was British-bred Can. and Am. Ch. Vederwolk of Vorden, obtained from the Conwood Kennel in Canada. Ch. Dusky Devil in turn, sired five champions.

From this point on, a succession of top winners from Mr. and Mrs. Fred Greenwood's great Wistonia Kennel in England were imported by Flakkee. These imports made spectacular ring history for Keeshonden in the United States, and were the basis for Flakkee's successful efforts to exhibit and produce true-to-type Keeshonden in accordance with the standard, through selective line-breeding of dogs of proven show quality.

Eng. Ch. Whimsy of Wistonia came to Flakkee in 1949 and was the first Keeshond bitch to take Best in Show in America. In fact, she topped two shows, won 15 BOB, 5 Groups and 9 other Group placings, and was the first Keeshond to place in the Group at Westminster (GR3). Whimsy is believed to have been the only Keeshond undefeated in breed competition in both England and the United States. She also was the dam of six Flakkee champions, and her daughter, Flakkee Sensation, who was by Eng. and Am. Ch. Wylco of Wistonia, had five champion Flakkee offspring sired by the kennel's imported Eng., Am. and Can. Ch. Wrocky of Wistonia. In the Wrocky/Sensation litter, the three males shown were Group win-

124

Ch. Patriot van Fitz, the first American-bred Keeshond to go Best in Show in the United States (1948). Patriot, by Ch. Clovelly Kris ex Ch. Kenise van Fitz, was bred by Vera Fitzpatrick and was owned by Flakkee Kennels.

Best in Show Brace (California): Ch. Tom Tit of Evenlode and son, Ch. Van Fitz Bingo. Owners: Vera and Kenneth Fitzpatrick

ners and included Ch. Cornelius Wrocky Selznick. But more about him later.

Whimsy was joined in 1951 by Eng. and Am. Ch. Wrona of Wistonia. Wrona also took a Best in Show, 8 Groups, and 10 other placings. Whimsy's and Wrona's winnings still stand as the records for Keeshond bitches in this country.

Other Flakkee imports in the 1950s were Eng. and Am. Ch. Waarborg of Wistonia, Eng. and Am. Ch. Wylco of Wistonia, and Am. Ch. Worrall of Wistonia. Worrall was sixth in the Phillips System Rating of the Top Ten Non-Sporting Dogs for 1959. The combined score of these imports brought 13 more BIS, 61 Group Firsts, and 62 other Group placings to the records of Flakkee-owned Kees, and their stud records were also impressive. Waarborg sired 10 AKC champions, Wylco 14 and Worrall 4. Eng. and Am. Ch. Wistonia Aristocrat of Doral was the father of five more.

In 1955, the Washingtons brought over Eng. and Am. Ch. Wylco's British-bred son, Eng. Ch. Wrocky of Wistonia, and his career in this country was to become legendary. Shown for only 11 months, Eng. Am. and Can. Ch. Wrocky of Wistonia in 36 times shown won 18 BIS (3 Canadian), 35 BOB, 33 Group Firsts, and 2 Seconds. This spectacular record in so short a time stands as an unsurpassed achievement in the breed.

Though not widely used at stud, Wrocky sired 12 champions. He will also go down in history for his importance as the direct ancestor of later generations of American-bred Kees who were top-flight Best in Show, Group and Specialty winners in the 1960s. Ch. Wrocky sired Flakkee's homebred Ch. Cornelius Wrocky Selznick, who had eight champion get. Wrocky was the grandsire of Ch. Flakee Sweepstakes, the great-grandsire of Am. and Can. Ch. Nederlan Herman v. Mack, and the great-great-grandsire of Ch. Von Storm's Emerson Prince Peit.

Ch. Cornelius Wrocky Selznick became, in 1963, the first American-bred Keeshond to place in the Top Ten of all Non-Sporting breeds in the Phillips System Ratings. To fully appreciate the significance of a Keeshond attaining that status, it must be realized that the breed was competing in the Non-Sporting Group with Miniature and Standard Poodles, whose annual registrations were then over 140,000, while yearly Keeshond registrations were still under 1,000. As a result, there was a preponderant number of Group and BIS-

Eng. Am. Can. Ch. Wrocky of Wistonia (Eng. Ch. Wylco of Wistonia ex Waneta of Wistonia). Breeder: Wistonia Kennels, England. Owner: Flakkee Kennels, 1958.

Mr. Porter Washington with: Eng. Am. Ch. Whimsy of Wistonia, the first Keeshond bitch to take Best in Show in America (1949), and dam of 8 champions: and Eng. Am. Ch. Wrona of Wistonia, the only other Keeshond bitch to win Best in Show in America (1951). Breeder: Wistonia Kennels, England. Owner: Flakkee Kennels.

127

winning Poodles to contend with, along with the other Non-Sporting breeds, before a Keeshond could even win the Group, and have a chance to take Best in Show. Nevertheless, a notable number of Ch. Wrocky of Wistonia's descendants have figured in the nation's Top Ten Non-Sporting. The success of Ch. Cornelius in the West made him fifth best Non-Sporting in 1963, eighth in 1964, and fifth in 1965. Meanwhile, Ch. Nederlan Herman was placing tenth in 1964 and ninth in 1965 and 1966, and Ch. Von Storm's Prince Peit was ninth in 1967.

The Washingtons' Ch. Flakkee Sweepstakes, or "Sweeper" as he has been called at home and in the dog show world, was well named. This great son of Ch. Cornelius Wrocky Selznick out of Elizabeth P. Yost's Flakkee Raffle Rain Check, swept through the shows to heights never before attained by a Keeshond in American rings.

Ch. Sweepstakes started his rise as the 1966 Phillips Ratings' tenth Best Non-Sporting Dog. In 1967 and 1968, his Group and Best in Show records made him the Top Non-Sporting Dog in the U.S. In both years he was also the winner of the Quaker Oats Award for the highest number of Non-Sporting Group wins, the first time a Keeshond had been a repeat winner of the Award. In addition, "Sweeper" was the first Keeshond to receive the Best Western Non-Sporting Dog citation in the Kennel Review contest for 1967. The next year he was again voted the Group honor, and named the Best Western Show Dog (of All Breeds) west of the Mississippi. But that's not all. In the 1968 Phillips tabulations, Sweepstakes was the second highest winning of all show dogs, all breeds, in the country.

In all, "Sweeper" added 46 Bests in Show, 109 Group Firsts, and 48 other Group placements to Flakkee's unparalleled record. The kennel's breeding record is equally important. Flakkee's imported and homebred studs and bitches have contributed 75 champions to the breed.

The Washingtons' roster of Specialty winners is particularly outstanding. After the Pacific Coast Club was re-established in 1950 as the Keeshond Club of Southern California, its Historian's records show that Flakkee entries topped eight of the club's Specialties. The winners were Chs. Waarborg of Wistonia, Wylco of Wistonia, Flakkee Wrock'n Roll, Cornelius Wrocky Selznick (twice) and Flakkee Sweepstakes (twice). In 1969, Mary Stetler's young Ch. Stetler's Derby Stakes, sired by Ch. Sweepstakes, took BOB at the show over 84

Eng. Am. Ch. Wylco of Wistonia
(Eng. Ch. Winchell of Wistonia
ex Eng. Ch. Wazelaine of Wistonia). Breeder: Wistonia Kennels, England. Owner: Flakkee
Kennels 1953.

Ch. Worrall of Wistonia (Eng.
Am. Ch. Wistonia Aristocrat of
Dorol ex Wakima of Wistonia).
Breeder, Wistonia Kennels, England. Owner, Flakkee Kennels
1958.

Eng. Am. Ch. Waarborg of Wistonia (Worthy of Wistonia ex
Eng. Ch. Anna of Vanloen).
Breeder: Wistonia Kennels, England. Owner: Flakkee Kennels
1950.

Ch. Cornelius Wrocky Selznick (Eng. Am. Can. Ch. Wrocky of Wistonia ex Flakkee Sensation), wh. 1960. Breeder-owner: Flakkee Kennels.

Ch. Flakkee Jackpot (Ch. Worrall of Wistonia ex Misty Volmaakt Beschermer), wh. 1966. Breeders: Mr. and Mrs. James Merchant. Owners: Flakkee Kennels.

Ch. Flakkee Sweepstakes (Ch. Cornelius Wrocky Selznick ex Flakkee Raffle Rain Check), wh. 1964. Breeder: Elizabeth P. Yost. Owner: Flakkee Kennels.

entries. "Sweeper's" wins included the 1967 Keeshond Club of Delaware Valley Specialty over 128 Kees, under judge Huig van Wingerden from Holland, and the Capital Keeshond Club Specialty in Washington, D.C. over another large entry.

Ch. Flakkee Jackpot, whelped in 1966 (by Ch. Worrall of Wistonia ex Misty Vomaakt Beschermer), bred by James and Caroline Merchant, was the next great Flakkee star. Jackpot's 12th BIS and 29th Group win brought the wins by Flakkee-bred or -owned Kees to a monumental 100 Bests in Show and 300 Groups—a world record for a Keeshonden kennel.

Mr. and Mrs. Washington's aims have been to exhibit dogs of merit and to breed only for quality. To that end, they have discerningly chosen their breeding stock, limited their program to an average of only two litters a year, and after weaning, the puppies are raised in their breeder's home. The results, on all counts, speak for themselves, and show how much Flakkee's superlative achievements, based on the great Wistonia imports and judicious line-breeding, have done for the Keeshond's present and future in America.

Mr. and Mrs. A. J. Kaufmann of Van Nuys, California, have been steadfast Keeshond devotees for many years. Mrs. Kaufmann recalls that her grandmother, Mrs. B. M. Rehm, raised and sold white Wolfsspitz to members of the nobility in Germany around 1875. The Kaufmanns first used Van Rehm in naming their Kees in the United States, and later changed to Ajkeer, a prefix which became well-known in West Coast shows.

Mrs. Kaufmann also relates that their first puppy, Fenna II Van Fitz, by Ch. Guelder Wiegbold ex Black-Eyed Susan Van Fitz, was purchased from Mrs. Fitzpatrick in 1941. Though Fenna was not a show dog, being 20 inches in height, she was beautifully marked and a wonderful pet, and in her second litter whelped the Kaufmanns' first two champions in 1948. They were by the George Davises' Ch. Beau Beau Van Fitz of Clovelly and were probably the first Kees puppies on TV when the litter was featured on Paramount Studio's Frank Goss Show.

Flakkee Tulip Time, a bitch puppy by Ch. Patriot Van Fitz ex Can. and Am. Ch. Vederwolk of Vorden, came to Ajkeer in 1949 from the Flakkee Kennel. Bred to Flakkee's Eng. and Am. Ch. Waarborg of Wistonia, Tulip Time added three titlists to the Kaufmanns' records. From then on, through the 1950s and '60s, many Ajkeer-bred winners such as Chs. Ajkeer Magic Hapi-Ladd II, Ajkeer Magic Sparkle, Ajkeer Wil-Wrock-Kim, and Ajkeer Weimar II were sired by the great English Wistonia dogs imported by Flakkee, or by the Kaufmanns' homebred studs or their British-bred Am. Ch. Weimar of Wistonia, purchased in America. And their Ch. Ajkeer Magic Sparkle (by Ch. Wylco of Wistonia ex Ch. Ajkeer Black Magic) won distinction as the dam of five champions.

Mrs. Kaufmann never bred any bitch more than three times, and there were usually from one to three owner-handled champions in the litters. Ever since the Kaufmanns started raising Kees, their selective breeding program has consistently contributed quality champions to the breed's progress.

Mr. and Mrs. Kaufmann were charter members of the Pacific Coast Keeshond Club, and when it became The Keeshond Club of Southern California in 1950, Mr. Kaufmann was a vice-president. Mrs. Kaufmann served the club in many capacities including membership on the Board of Directors. During her term as president, 1964–1965, she initiated show-handling classes and inclusion of a Puppy Sweepstake in the club's Specialty at Long Beach, which had a record West Coast entry for the breed up to that time.

Mrs. Gladys Baldwin joined the Keeshond boosters and breeders in southern California in 1947 when she obtained Mrs. Fitzpatrick's Wilhelmina Van Fitz, and started her successful Van Bie Kennel. Wilhelmina was by Clovelly Kris ex Ch. Kenise Van Fitz, and bred to Ch. Conwood Kurt (from Canada) produced the first Van Bie litter. One of the litter which made a unique record for herself, her breeder, and the breed, was Van Bie Berna.

Berna whelped 12 puppies in one litter by the Fitzpatrick's imported Eng. and Am. Ch. Tom Tit of Evenlode. Anyone who has raised an average-sized litter of six knows how much personal attention and stamina is required from both the dam and the breeder. But Berna and Mrs. Baldwin came through with flying colors. Between them, every puppy grew to sturdy maturity, three finished, and many others won numerous points toward their titles.

The caliber of the Kees produced by Mrs. Baldwin's quite limited breeding activity has contributed more than 25 champions and many Obedience winners to the breed. Some of the best known champions bringing renown to the Van Bie name throughout the United States were: Van Bie Rikki; Van Fitz Mr. Bie; Wilene First Knight; Jason of Van Bie (by Ch. Van Bie Rikki ex Roxi v. Keesdale), bought and exhibited by Mrs. Attrude Apsey of Detroit; and Mrs. Apsey's Ch. Van Bie Lucky Clover (by Ch. Armel Jeremias ex Ch. Van Bie Berta), winner of the Keeshond Club of Delaware Valley's 115-entry Specialty in 1963. In the Obedience trials, Van Bie Ponderosa Koningen UD, owned and handled by Thomas J. Ballen of Denver, was the top winning Obedience Keeshond in the country in 1967 and 1968.

When the Pacific Coast Club became the Keeshond Club of Southern California, Mrs. Baldwin was elected secretary-treasurer. She subsequently moved to northern California, where she was active as an early member of the Nor-Cal Club, formed in 1961. In 1965, Mrs. Baldwin had the distinction of judging the first Keeshond Club of America Puppy Futurity Stake.

The first Keeshond in the Frank Ketchams' Rocky Falls Kennel was Kingleigh's Headlight, bought from Louis Todd's Kingleigh Kennel in Indiana in 1950. The next was Vikeland's Duchess, from the Vikeland Kennel in Kerman, California. The Ketchams' first litter, in 1953, was out of Dutchess, and was sired by Jan Anton Van Den Krashof, a Dutch import owned by the Keesdale Kennel in Grass Valley, California.

Mrs. Ketcham's own account relates how they showed their Kees from 1954 to 1958 in many nearby shows in northern California, but since—in many instances—theirs were the only Keeshonden shown, there were no major wins. They "exhibited a number of dogs solely to determine their show potential prior to sale", and "from 1956 to 1962, sometimes had 50 to 60 grown dogs and puppies at one time."

In 1960, Colonel Applejack of Carmel was finished to American and Canadian championships. Mr. and Mrs. Norman Cory started exhibiting their Gallant Imp in 1967, and showed five others to their titles for the Ketchams. And Mrs. Ketcham attributes another five champions, owned by others, as being "of the Rocky Falls breeding". Mr. Cory became president of the Nor-Cal Keeshond Club in 1967.

Mr. and Mrs. Floyd Matthews of Modesto, California, had at one time bred and shown Chow Chows as a hobby. Years later, when they were without a dog, they studied dog magazines looking for another breed with beauty and brains and decided on the Keeshond. Only knowing the breed from pictures of show dogs, they were pretty startled when—in 1957—they received by plane a puppy who was at that gangly, all-legs-and-ears and short puppy-coat stage. But in a few

Ch. Ruttkay Go Man Go, CD
(Ch. Karel of Altnavanog ex
Ruttkay Romance), wh. 1957.
Breeder: Virginia Ruttkay. Owners: Blanche and Floyd
Matthews, Modesto Kennels.

Ch. Ajkeer Magic Sparkle (Ch. Wylco
of Wistonia ex Ch. Ajkeer Black
Magic), wh. 1953. Dam of 5 champions. Breeder-owners: Mr. and Mrs.
A. J. Kaufmann, Ajkeer Kennels.

Best in Show Brace, California:
Ch. Mr. Van Sandar of Modesto
and sire, Ch. Ruttkay Go Man
Go, CD. Owners: Blanche and
Floyd Matthews, Modesto Kennels.

135

months he was beautiful and soon gained his title as Ch. Ruttkay Go Man Go (by Ch. Karel of Altnavanog ex Ruttkay Romance). Mr. Matthews took him through CD in three straight trials, and in limited showing in conformation had some Group placings. Bred to only eight bitches, Go Man Go sired 12 champions out of four of them.

Meanwhile, the Matthews had obtained two bitches for their Modesto Kennel. One was Mrs. Cummings II's Dirdon's Leise Van Hanzel (by Ch. Hanzel Van Dohrmann CD ex Ch. Dirdon's Legacy v. Hocage CD), and the other was Flakkee Contessa from the Porter Washingtons. The only four puppies shown from the Ch. Contessa-Go Man Go litter finished in a flash. One of them was Ch. Mr. Van Sandar of Modesto who, bred to Dirdon's Leise, produced Ch. Miss Tom Tit of Modesto.

Mrs. Matthews' report cites as a highlight for Modesto Kees, the 1963 Golden Gate show's Best Brace in Show win by her owner-handled Ch. Go Man Go with his son, Ch. Mr. Van Sandar, and their repeat of the win at that year's Oakland show. But there was an even greater triumph to come.

Ch. Junior Miss of Modesto was bred to Kenneth Fitzpatrick's imported Am. Ch. Vertuuren of Vorden, and whelped Van Fitz The Strutter of Modesto, co-owned and bred by Floyd Matthews and Dr. L. C. Buente. From the classes, The Strutter topped the 1968 Keeshond Club of Delaware Valley Specialty over the 117 Kees present (including 22 champions) under Jere Collins from England, and went on to Second in the Group. The Strutter completed his title in short time in Eastern competition, and received some Group wins before going home to California.

Ever since the Nor-Cal Keeshond Club was organized in 1961, Mrs. Matthews has been its staunch supporter and secretary. In addition, the Matthews' Kees have figured in the success of other owners in northern California.

The careers of Keeshonden as show dogs and producers are historically important. But something equally important, namely how much Kees mean to their owners, is reflected in the stories of two Nor-Cal Club members, sent to us by Mrs. Matthews.

After losing her childhood pet from hepatitis in 1952, Mrs. Lewis Cuccia of Richmond vowed she would sometime have another Keeshond to love. Her wish came true in 1961, and the Cuccias raised two litters. Their Gingerbread Boy CD was in the first. The second was out of Gingerbread's sister, who was mated to Ch. Go Man Go, and produced Sal-Mae's Tom Thumb CD. In 1967, the Cuccias' owner-handled Tom Thumb and Gingerbread Boy carried off the Richmond KC show's top honors as Best Brace in Show.

Mr. and Mrs. Theodore Bosworth fell in love with this beautiful breed in 1960 and set out to find a Keeshond of their own. About a year later they saw a puppy named Silver Lady of Dutch Meer and bought her on the spot from Mrs. Zelotes Baker. The Bosworths trained and showed their pet to her championship and CD title. Silver Lady was bred to Ch. Go Man Go, and two of the litter that the Bosworths kept for pets grew up to be their proud breeder-owner-handled Ch. Shaund Kee O'Dutch Meer and Ch. Teddy Bear of Dutch Meer CD. The Bosworths have also been active in the Nor-Cal Club, Mr. Bosworth having served as a director and vice-president, and Mrs. Bosworth as chairman of important committees.

Other Nor-Cal Club members listed by Mrs. Matthews as having one or more champions are: Mrs. Jean Bruce, Jerralee Gomes, the Arthur Waldos, the Wm. Conners, Mrs. Shirley Gray, and Mr. and Mrs. P. E. Brakebill, Jr.

Muisjes van Hondenhok CD came to Mr. and Mrs. Ralph Sims as a spayed bitch from the Santa Cruz Animal Shelter in 1960. She was followed the next year, from the same source, by Zee's Zealous Imp, a "teen-age" male. These two Kees, which had been abandoned through no fault of their own, were the Sims' introduction to the breed and led to their raising Keeshonden with the Zeedrift prefix. Ch. Phaedra Zuider Kee, by Coventry's Baron Zuider Kee ex Mishka of Willawalt, was purchased from her breeder, Mrs. W. J. Bayne, and was a factor in Zeedrift's breeding plans.

Zee's Zealous Imp completed CD and in 1963 quickly obtained his conformation title. The Sims bought a male from a litter Ch. Zee's Imp had previously sired. The puppy grew up to be Ch. Echo's Onzin van Hondenhok CD, and sired their Ch. Zeedrift Kwikzilver, a winner of a number of Groups and a Best in Show, who also topped the big entry at the Nor-Cal Club's first Specialty.

Mr. and Mrs. Sims were active in Nor-Cal Club affairs during their membership and the Keeshond Club of America later appointed them National Publicity Chairmen for 1969.

Mrs. Richard Stark's first sight of a Keeshond puppy in 1959, when she was 16 years old, convinced her that she must have one. After her marriage, she purchased Prince Kodi of Rocky Falls in 1962. Then to keep Kodi company, came a "clumsy, careening seven-month-old puppy registered Boko", bred by Gary Heymann. Both dogs went to Obedience school. Kodi was the class star, and went on to complete his CDX in three straight shows. Boko also eventually got his CD, but proved his truer mettle as a showdog, winning his championship and a Group and siring two champions. One was the Starks' Ch. Star-Kee Forever Amber, who was out of their Zeedrift Aanvalig Plump-Lump, obtained from the Sims' first litter.

Mrs. Stark was a former member and past president of the Nor-Cal Club, and has served on the Keeshond Club of America's national Code of Ethics Committee.

Mr. and Mrs. Chester Pierce of San Francisco have been devoted to Kees for over a decade, and in limited breeding have raised good winners with their K.C. prefix. In 1957 they acquired the late Mrs. Fitzpatrick's imported Whinchat of Evenlode. Mr. Fitzpatrick owned and showed the Pierces' homebred Ch. Van Fitz Princess Liz in the late 1960s and the Pierces sold their Ch. K.C.'s Holland Dutchess to Mr. and Mrs. Walter Dayringer in San Ramon.

From Dutchess' litter sired by Ch. Ruttkay Go Man Go, the Day-ringers kept two males and a bitch. Those three soon became Ch. Jul-Day Von Diedrick UD, Ch. Jul-Day Ravensdown de Syl UD, and Ch. Jul-Day Wunderlust de Sylvia UD. A unique record—three from one litter with both their championship and UD titles!

Ch. Wunderlust was among the three top winning Obedience Kees in the United States in 1966 and 1967, and was important as a dam. Her litter by British-bred Ch. Vangabang of Vorden produced Chs. Jul-Day Smokelaar and Jul-Day Snoodark (who we have seen became a BIS and Group winner in his short ring career under Mr. Fitzpatrick's ownership).

In addition to their success as breeders of show dogs and owner-bred and handled Obedience stars, Mr. and Mrs. Dayringer were voted by the Keeshond Club of America to receive the 1968 *Dog World Award* in recognition of their "outstanding service, accomplishment, and activity in behalf of dogs and better care for all dogs".

When the Dayringers heard that a large number of Keeshonden had been abandoned in a so-called "breeder's" backyard without food or water, they swung into action. By the time they reached the starving animals many miles away, the dogs were in serious condition and the owner could not be located. Through local humane authorities, the Dayringers had the Kees legally impounded and given their first food and water in over a week. They were then officially released to the Dayringers, who, with a veterinarian's supervision, personally nursed the 13 survivors back to physical and emotional health—an ordeal which took many weeks of work and much expense, but which had a happy ending. After countless more weeks of effort finding appropriate homes, Mr. and Mrs. Dayringer placed each of the abandoned Kees as the pets of devoted owners.

All that dogs have contributed to the welfare of mankind through the ages can never be repaid in full. But Mr. and Mrs. Dayringer's rescue and rehabilitation of these helpless victims of human cruelty are shining examples of what people who care can do to help suffering animals.

APPEARANCE: Well-balanced, short-coupled, compact; luxurious coat, plume, mane, "trousers"; gait sharp, brisk

SKULL well-proportioned to body, wedge-shaped

STOP definite

EYES dark brown; medium sized; oblique; not too wide apart

TEETH white, sound, strong, upper overlap lower slightly

MOUTH neither over nor undershot; lips black, close meeting; without corner wrinkles

MUZZLE dark, medium length, neither coarse nor snipy; well-proportioned to skull

CHEST deep, strong

FORELEGS straight, well-feathered

COLOR mixture of gray, black; undercoat, pale gray or cream; outer, black-tipped; no pronounced white; light gray shoulder line markings well-defined

SIZE: Height, ideal, males, 18"; females, 17"; size should not outweigh type; from withers to rump equal to height

HEAD: Face foxlike; hair smooth, soft, short; texture velvety; expression dependent on "spectacles" (delicately penciled lines slanting slightly upward from outer corners of eyes to lower corner of ears); distinct markings and shadings form short, expressive eyebrows. Absence, a fault

EARS small, triangular; mounted high on head; carried erect; very dark; covered with thick, velvety short hair; length in proportion to head

NECK moderately long, well-shaped, well-set-on shoulders; mane profuse

BACK short; straight; sloping to hindquarters slightly

TAIL—set high; moderately long, well feathered, tightly curled over back; flat, close to body; gray plume on top when curled; tip black

HIND LEGS profusely feathered to hocks; bone good; cream colored

HOCKS slightly bent

FEET compact, well-rounded, catlike; cream colored; toes arched; nails black

COAT abundant, straight, harsh, standing out; undercoat thick, downy; no parting down back

TUCK-UP moderate

RIBS well-ribbed, barrel well-rounded

6

Official Breed Standard of the Keeshond

As adopted by the Keeshond Club of America, and approved by the American Kennel Club, July 12, 1949.

GENERAL APPEARANCE AND CONFORMATION

The Keeshond is a handsome dog, of well-balanced, short coupled body, attracting attention not only by his alert carriage and intelligent expression, but also by his luxurious coat, his richly plumed tail, well curled over his back, and by his foxlike face and head with small pointed ears. His coat is very thick round the neck, fore part of the shoulders and chest, forming a lionlike mane. His rump and hind legs, down to the hocks, are also thickly coated, forming the characteristic "trousers." His head, ears and lower legs are covered with thick short hair. The ideal height of fully matured dogs (over 2 years old), measured from top of withers to the ground, is: for males, 18 inches; bitches, 17 inches. However, size consideration should not outweigh that of type. When dogs are judged equal in type, the dog nearest the ideal height is to be preferred. Length of back from withers to rump should equal height as measured above.

HEAD

Expression—Expression is largely dependent on the distinctive characteristic called "spectacles"—a delicately penciled line slanting slightly upward from the outer corner of each eye to the lower corner of the ear, coupled with distinct markings and shadings forming short but expressive eyebrows. Markings (or shadings) on face and head must present a pleasing appearance, imparting to the dog an alert and intelligent expression. *Fault*—Absence of "spectacles".

Skull—The head should be well-proportioned to the body, wedge-shaped when viewed from above. Not only in muzzle, but the whole head should give this impression when the ears are drawn back by covering the nape of the neck and the ears with one hand. Head in profile should exhibit a definite stop. *Fault*—Apple head, or absence of stop.

Muzzle—The muzzle should be dark in color and of medium length, neither coarse nor snipy, and well-proportioned to the skull.

Mouth—The mouth should be neither overshot nor undershot. Lips should be black and closely meeting, not thick, coarse, or sagging; and with no wrinkle at the corner of the mouth. *Fault*—Overshot or undershot.

Teeth—The teeth should be white, sound and strong (but discoloration from distemper not to penalize severely) ; upper teeth should just overlap the lower teeth.

Eyes—Eyes should be dark brown in color, of medium size, rather oblique in shape and not set too wide apart. *Fault*—Protruding round eyes or eyes light in color.

Ears—Ears should be small, triangular in shape, mounted high on head and carried erect; dark in color and covered with thick, velvety, short hair. Size should be proportionate to the head—length approximating the distance from outer corner of the eyes to the nearest edge of the ear. *Fault*—Ears not carried erect when at attention.

BODY

Neck and Shoulders—The neck should be moderately long, well-shaped and well-set on shoulders; covered with a profuse mane, sweeping from under the jaw and covering the whole of the front part of the shoulders and chest, as well as the top part of the shoulders.

Chest, Back and Loin—The body should be compact with a short, straight back sloping slightly downward toward the hindquarters; well-ribbed, barrel well rounded, belly moderately tucked up, deep and strong of chest.

Legs—Forelegs should be straight seen from any angle and well feathered. Hindlegs should be profusely feathered down to the hocks —not below, with hocks only slightly bent. Legs must be of good bone and cream in color. *Fault*—Black markings below the knee, penciling excepted.

Feet—The feet should be compact, well-rounded, catlike, and cream in color. Toes are nicely arched, with black nails. *Fault*— White foot or feet.

Tail—The tail should be set on high, moderately long, and well-feathered, tightly curled over back. It should lie flat and close to the body with a very light gray plume on top where curled, but the tip of the tail should be black. The tail should form a part of the "silhouette" of the dog's body, rather than give the appearance of an appendage. *Fault*—Tail not lying close to the back.

Action—Dogs should show boldly and keep tails curled over the back. They should move cleanly and briskly; and the movement should be straight and sharp (not lope like a German Shepherd Dog). *Fault*—Tail not carried over back when moving.

COAT

The body should be abundantly covered with long, straight, harsh hair; standing well out from a thick, downy undercoat. The hair on the legs should be smooth and short, except for a feathering on the front legs and "trousers", as previously described, on the hindlegs. The hair on the tail should be profuse, forming a rich plume. Head, including muzzle, skull and ears, should be covered with smooth, soft, short hair—velvety in texture on the ears. Coat must not part down the back. *Fault*—Silky, wavy, or curly coats. Part in coat down the back.

143

COLOR AND MARKINGS

A mixture of gray and black. The undercoat should be very pale gray or cream (not tawny). The hair of the outer coat is black tipped, the length of the black tips producing the characteristic shading of color. The color may vary from light to dark, but any pronounced deviation from the gray color is not permissible. The plume of the tail should be very light gray when curled on back, and the tip of the tail should be black. Legs and feet should be cream. Ears should be very dark—almost black. Shoulder line markings (light gray) should be well defined. The color of the ruff and "trousers" is generally lighter than that of the body. "Spectacles" and shadings, as previously described, are characteristic of the breed and must be present to some degree. There should be no pronounced white markings. *Very Serious Faults*—Entirely black or white or any other solid color; any pronounced deviation from the gray color.

SCALE OF POINTS

General Conformation and Appearance			20
Head			
Shape	6		
Eyes	5		
Ears	5		
Teeth	4		
		....	20
Body			
Chest, Back and Loin	10		
Tail	10		
Neck and Shoulders ..	8		
Legs	4		
Feet	3		
		....	35
Coat			15
Color and Markings			10
		TOTAL	100

144

7

Blueprint of the Keeshond

THE *Description and Standard of Points* adopted by the Keeshond Club of America and approved by the American Kennel Club is the official, written "blueprint" of the ideal Keeshond by which the breed is judged in the United States. It is based mainly on the British Standard. The American Standard is a bit more detailed, but in essentials they are the same.

Thorough study of the Standard on pages 141, together with study of the pictorial depiction on page 140 and the illustration of "Rights and Wrongs" on pages 147–149 is important for everyone who now raises and shows Kees, or who may do so in the future.

The spoken and written words of today are quite an improvement over our prehistoric ancestors' grunts, gestures and picture writing. Even so, the jargon used in such specialized fields as dog breeding, exhibiting, and judging can be downright baffling, especially for newcomers. The fact that many words mean different things to different people, adds to the confusion. Colors are difficult to describe. Indefinite phrases in standards like "moderately long neck", "slightly bent hocks", etc. are subject to individual interpretations. For example, how slight is "slightly"? It is almost as vague as the oldie, "How high is up?"

Fortunately, in comparison to those of many other breeds, the Keeshond standard is exceptionally clear and complete. Nevertheless, there are important fundamental subjects in judging the overall quality of dogs, whether in the rings or at home, that must be considered in conjunction with all standards. These subjects are *"Balance"*, *"Soundness"*, and *"Type"*. Just what do these words mean as applied to dogs, and specifically to Keeshonden?

Balance

When a dog is well-balanced, each part of the animal is in harmonious proportion to all of its other parts and in accordance with the conformation called for in the specific breed's Standard. For example, a Keeshond may have a perfect head, but if the head seems too small or too large in relation to the body, the dog lacks balance.

Another factor in regard to balance or lack of it in a Keeshond is the neck, vaguely described in the Standard as "moderately long, well-shaped and well-set on shoulders". To clarify the description, the author submits that the neck should be set far enough back on the shoulders and be long enough to form an arch or "crest" as it is called, so that when the dog is at attention, the back of the skull is in line with the backs of the front legs. (See illustrated Standard.)

A short neck, or one not based well back and thrust forward, is a deterrent to a properly-balanced appearance. This is usually accompanied by a faulty "top-line", i.e. a level back or one which slopes downward toward the withers (top of the shoulders). These structural faults make a dog seem to pitch forward instead of correctly sloping from the withers down toward the hindquarters, and breeders should—through selective breeding—make every effort to breed them out.

Where the Keeshond's tail is based, and how it is carried, are also vital to a balanced effect because the tail must be part of the breed's silhouette. The tail's base should be well forward from the rear protuberance of the pelvic bone (rump), and the whole tail lie curled absolutely flat on the back, the tighter the curl the better. It should never seem to be an appendage held either up in a loop above the back or hanging off the dog's rear.

146

Keeshond Rights and Wrongs

Photographs by Evelyn Shafer

These depictions were first presented in August 1963 issue of Popular Dogs, *Philadelphia, U.S.A., and are included here with special permission.*

A well-balanced Keeshond head; note "spectacles," stop, shape of eye, ear placement, muzzle proportion.

Eyes should be oblique—never round and not too wide apart; this round eye should be faulted.

A poor head; note light muzzle marking, light eyes and lack of "spectacles."

Another poor head; note the too-wide-set ears, also the light eyes; both detract from expression. Ears too big; insufficient ruff.

147

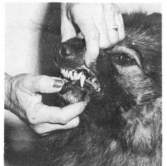

An excellent bite, upper teeth just overlap lower.

An extremely poor head, completely lacking "spectacles." Note insufficient stop; muzzle is too long.

An excellent front.

A "fiddle" front; wrong.

Poor; flat feet, bowed front.

Front too narrow; poor.

A good rear; good tail placement and plume; feet good; note short back.

Note straight stifle; poor tail carriage, no plume; lacking "trousers."

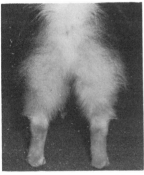

A good, sturdy rear with good bone.

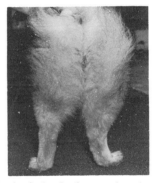

Cowhocked (hocks turning in and feet out) ; a poor one.

A poor foot, neither compact nor rounded; down on pasterns.

An overlong body with a topline too straight; topline should slope from shoulder to rump; wavy coat on back is wrong, as are the poor pasterns.

149

Soundness

The question of which is more important, "type" or "soundness" in dogs seems to be a recurring subject of discussion among both novice and experienced dog fanciers in all breeds. In this writer's opinion—as a breeder, exhibitor, and AKC judge—"right type" and "typey" signify that a dog is correctly representative of its particular breed, and in conformity with all points of the Standard, including temperament. Judges and knowledgeable exhibitors advisedly put great emphasis on the necessity of a dog being "sound", which in show parlance specifically applies to its physical structure and the resultant "action" (gait) and stance. The author's view is that if a dog is correctly constructed as required in the Standard, it moves and stands accordingly. Therefore, soundness is actually an inherent part of right type.

In regard to legs and action, the Keeshond standard states: "Forelegs should be straight, seen from any angle." On the hindlegs, "hocks should be only slightly bent." Moreover, "Dogs should show boldly and keep tails curled over the back. They should move cleanly and briskly, and the movement should be straight and sharp (not lope like a German Shepherd Dog) ". This is all very well as far as it goes, but let us look into the important matter of what contributes to sound action and stance.

When moving and standing, front feet and legs should turn neither in nor out. Elbows should be close to the body. The pasterns, i.e. the wrists, should not bend backwards, and the legs should be straight and at right angles to the feet. Weak pasterns are a prevalent fault in Kees which breeders should earnestly try to eliminate.

On the hindlegs, what appear to be the elbows are actually the dog's true heels, and are called the hocks. Viewed from the rear and side when standing, the hindlegs from the hocks down should be straight, parallel to each other and at right angles to the ground. "Spread" hocks turn outward, a defect that contributes to hind feet coming too close together or overlapping when moving. Hocks should *never* point or swing toward each other at any time. This is a disfiguring malformation known as "cow-hocks". Cow-hocked Keeshonden of any age should be definitely avoided as breeding or show prospects. Angulation at the hock joints should be sufficient for a Keeshond to trot freely without stiffness or roll in its gait. Proper action also requires that all four legs move straight forward in line with the direction of travel. When that is not the case, the fault is described as "crabbing" or "side-wheeling".

Type

The true-to-type Keeshond, in accordance with the American standard, is a sturdily-built, medium-sized dog distinguished by its beauty and elegance. But we must face the fact that although American breeders have made great strides in developing uniformity of type, there are presently two types of Keeshonden in this country. One type is in line with the medium size and other physical characteristics of the ideal Keeshond designated in the Dutch, British and American standards, namely males 18 inches high at the top of the withers, and bitches 17 inches. The official American Kennel Club standard also says: "Size consideration should not outweigh that of type. When dogs are judged equal in type, the dog nearest the ideal height is to be preferred."

The German Wolfsspitz type is bigger than the ideal size, is proportionately coarse-headed and boned, and is often a lumbering, excessively-coated dog with big, bat-like ears. Mrs. Doreen Anderson, the British Keeshond breeder and judge, has aptly described such Kees as "heavy fur rugs on legs".

The following comments received by the author in 1955 from Mrs. Stanfert Kroese, of Helvoirt, Holland, a Dutch breed authority and a judge in Europe and England, point up the impact of size on type: "We in Holland have been trying to breed the Dutch Keeshond with more refined type and foxy heads as a separate breed from the German Wolfsspitz, which are larger and more wolfish in head. The standards of the two breeds are almost identical except that the German says '18 inches or higher, the higher the better', while the Dutch standard says 'not higher than 18 inches'. I want to stress that we have found it a mistake to breed Keeshonden too big, as the very big ones are apt to be coarse in head and expression and are clumsy movers, whereas the Keeshond should be a sturdy dog, but a very active one."

Among the reasons for the variance in type is the fact that most Kees in America have come from England, where early British imports of the medium-sized Keeshonden from Holland were com-

151

bined with the larger German Wolfsspitz (*Grosse Grau Spitz*) brought from Germany. Although basically the same breed, both types individually appear in later generations as a result of genetic laws.

The two types of Kees have been a problem discussed through many decades in Holland, Germany, England, and the United States. However, authorities on genetics have shown that one type *can* become established if breeders concentrate on it. Anything from giant to spindly-boned, undersized Keeshonden can be produced. Though our Standard does not describe size in terms of weight, it clearly defines the ideal height and correspondingly correct Keeshond. Therefore the future size and consequent type of Keeshond called for in the American Standard is the responsibility of everyone who raises a litter.

Color

Under Color and Markings our Standard states: "A mixture of gray and black. The undercoat should be very pale gray or cream (not tawny). The hair of the outer coat is black-tipped, the length of the black tips producing the characteristic shading of color. The color may vary from light to dark, but *any pronounced deviation from the gray color is not permissible.*" The italics are the author's.

The Standard's statement is clean-cut and easily understood. We all know the color of fresh cream and that very pale gray and very pale cream are almost white. The dictionary defines "tawny" as the color of a lion. The words italicized in the previous paragraph show that the *only* permissible coloring is of mixtures shading from almost white, through gray to black.

Head, Expression and Eye Color

All parts of a Keeshond's head should be in pleasing proportion to its own parts, and to the whole dog. The skull should be wedge-shaped and somewhat flat, never "domey". There should be a definite dent (or "stop" as it is called) between the eyes, just above where the skull seems to meet the muzzle. Inadequate stop is penalized. The muzzle should be of medium length in relation to the depth of

152

the skull, and be neither unattractively coarse nor so narrow as to be "snipey". (Bitches' muzzles are usually not as wide as males'.) The jaws must meet in front in a "scissors bite" with the upper teeth just overlapping the lower.

Small, triangular-shaped ears, mounted high on the head and carried absolutely erect at attention, are essential. When Kees are expressing happiness and affection they usually hold their ears folded back into the ruff. But ears should never droop or fold forward from the tips, and big ears, or those which point away from each other like a bat's, are unsightly, bad faults.

The Keeshond's expression is exceedingly important. According to the Standard it "is largely dependent on the distinctive characteristic called 'spectacles'—a delicately penciled line slanting slightly upward from the outer corner of each eye to the lower corner of the ear, coupled with distinct markings and shadings forming short but expressive eyebrows. FAULT: Absence of spectacles."

This description of face markings in the Standard sometimes confuses people. However, to visualize the effect, just imagine a pair of dark-rimmed spectacles (without a nose-piece) on the dog's face. In other words, light gray areas around the eyes are outlined by dark hair to delineate the spectacles' rims, and are joined by dark, penciled lines from the outer corners of the eyes toward the ears that might be considered the side-pieces.

The eyes play a vital part in the breed's typically gentle expression. They should be deep, dark brown, the darker the better, somewhat oval in shape and of medium size. If eyes are light colored or have a light band around a dark center, they have an ugly, glaring expression which is utterly untypical, and should be penalized accordingly, along with round, bulging eyes.

Coat

When in full bloom, at from two to three years old and on, the Keeshond is an arrestingly handsome breed, distinguished by the subtle shadings of palest gray to black which create the characteristic markings in its luxurious, off-standing coat. To achieve the right effect, the whole coat must be dense, consisting in reality of two coats—a thick, downy undercoat and very harsh, straight guard hairs as an outercoat. Silky, drooping, or wavy coats are faults.

Temperament

The typical Keeshond has an outgoing personality, a friendly attitude toward people and dogs, and is sensible and affectionate. Although these characteristics are not mentioned in the Standard, they are nonetheless essential in the typical Keeshond, and in the author's opinion, are more important than anything else. After all, who wants to have a timid or belligerent dog in the home or show ring? If a Keeshond does not have a good disposition in every way, it is not true to type.

Fortunately for the breed, conscientious breeders and knowledgeable judges in the United States have successfully stressed the necessity of maintaining the Keeshond's excellent temperament. But the breed's whole future in that respect is dependent upon the continuation of this stress.

Chris Blom

8

Choosing a Keeshond Puppy

I T is an exciting and important event when you buy a Keeshond because you are gaining a new member of your family.

For elderly people, and those of any age who live alone, a Keeshond in the house can make the difference between loneliness and having a devoted companion. For youngsters, Kees are jolly, gentle playmates whose main desire is to be loved and to please their owners. And when parents explain how and why dogs should be treated with kindness and understanding, children learn to be considerate of all living things, including people.

There are a number of things to think about when you acquire a dog. For instance, for the sake of harmony among the people in the home, and for the puppy's or older dog's own welfare, *everyone in the household should really want a dog,* and an adult should be responsible for the feeding, general care and house-training of the newcomer. To count on "Junior" or his little sister for those jobs is just wishful thinking. The ability of youngsters to do all that is needed is seldom adequate and their enthusiasm for looking after their new, live toy usually wears off in no time flat. The results can be unfortunate, and sometimes disastrous. The puppy may be neglected and become physically and emotionally miserable. Through no fault of its own, it may get into bad habits in the house, or wander off, be stolen, or even killed by a car, particularly if it is not safeguarded by an outdoor enclosure.

Keeshonden of all ages are exceptionally healthy, clean and eager to learn. But any dog can be harmfully affected by insufficient knowledgeable care and training, particularly when it is very young.

Before you choose your puppy, it is a sound idea to do some homework and make certain decisions. Study the official Keeshond Standard (page 141), and the Breeders' Code of Ethics (page 178). Obtain all possible information about the reliability of different breeders. Decide what age and sex you want, and why. Remember, each week of a puppy's life adds to its mental ability to learn what you want to teach it.

If you buy a male for a pet, don't expect that people who own females will come knocking at your door to use your dog as a mate for their bitch unless he has at least proved himself to have a certain amount of quality by becoming a champion. Even so, there are countless excellent Keeshond champions available at stud throughout the country.

If your pet is to be a female, and not to be used for breeding, it is far better for your bitch, your own convenience, and your relations with your neighbors, to have her spayed. This is a simple operation. She can be home from the veterinarian's in a few days, and contrary to popular belief, being spayed will not change her personality. Unless an unspayed female is put in a boarding kennel during her "season", the wind brings news of her condition to males for miles around. The dogs will surround your home day and night for about three weeks, howl and fight with each other, and their owners and other neighbors can justifiably file complaints against you with the community's officials. What's more, your unspayed female may get out of the house and as a result, present you with an unwanted litter of mongrel puppies to raise and find homes for.

Sources of Supply

For many reasons it is wise to deal directly with reputable breeders, and whenever possible, to go to the kennel and personally select the best puppy you can afford. After all, it costs no more—in fact, usually much less in time and money—to maintain a well-bred, healthy puppy of good quality than it does a mediocre or poor specimen. So you might just as well own one you can be proud of as a good example of the breed.

Fortunately for the buying public, there are a great many Keeshond breeders who are devoted to the breed and to the welfare of the dogs they sell. Above all other considerations, the objective of conscientious breeders is to raise healthy, good quality dogs with proper temperament, bred selectively with thought to the standard, and the laws of heredity. These breeders give personal care and attention to their dogs—an important contribution on all counts. They take pride in what they produce, and whenever desired, make every effort to be helpful to novice and other buyers.

The best way to locate responsible Keeshond breeders is through the American Kennel Club, 51 Madison Avenue, New York, N. Y. 10010. Among its many functions pertaining to purebred dogs, the AKC will give you the name and address of the secretary of The Keeshond Club of America. The national, or "parent" club as it is called, keeps an up-to-date listing of its member-breeders throughout the United States who have reported that they have Keeshonden for sale. And it should be noted that these breeders have signed the club's Breeders' Code of Ethics.

On receipt of your inquiry about available puppies or adult Kees, the national club's secretary will send you the current *Puppy List,* plus the name and location of the secretary of the local Keeshond club nearest you, from whom you can also obtain information about Keeshonden available from its members. (As you will see in Chapter 14, there are local Keeshond clubs in many parts of the country.)

On the other hand, there are people who raise litters from their pet females and dump the puppies at wholesale without concern for the ultimate buyers' fitness as dog owners. These so-called "breeders" are apparently more interested in money than in the welfare of the dogs they have produced. The same can also be said of the "puppy-mill" and "dog-farm" operators who raise dogs on a large scale as a money-making scheme. Far too often, the result of this type of callous attitude toward animals is that to reduce basic costs, the dogs may not have been properly wormed, inoculated, or nourished before being finally bought by inexperienced seekers of a pet. Even when puppies survive such inadequate early care, the veterinarians' bills that may pile up can make them costly investments for the eventual purchasers.

157

Minimum Age for Selection

Experienced breeders generally agree that from eight to twelve weeks old is a good age for appraisal of the potential quality of Keeshond puppies. By that time, the bone structure and other characteristics are fairly well discernible. But the statements of anyone who says that this or that particular puppy is definitely a future champion, should be taken with a large grain of salt.

To select a puppy from the usual Keeshond litter of from five to eight, can be quite baffling when you are faced with a whole group of rollicking, beautiful, silver-gray-to-black-shaded balls of fluff. So ask the breeder to only show you those of the sex in which you are interested, and that are available.

Health

The puppy you buy should have had a proper physical start in life. Before it leaves its first home, it should have been wormed, given the preventive inoculations against distemper, hepatitis and leptospirosis appropriate to its age. And assuming that it had been weaned at six weeks or earlier, it should for some time have been on a balanced diet of meat, vitamins, cod liver oil, calcium, milk and cereal. This is one of the many reasons why breeders who consider the welfare of their puppies will not deliver dogs under eight weeks old. And if the hazards of shipping are involved, delivery is usually postponed until about four months of age. So, if your dog is being shipped, be patient and grateful that the breeder has your and the puppy's interests at heart.

A healthy puppy is full of vim. Its eyes are clear, not bloodshot, and have no discharge. The nose is clean, cool and slightly moist, not dry. Bowel movements are formed, not runny. The coat stands out from the body and has a fluffy, lively appearance with no flaky skin or black granules of flea dirt. The little dog should be plump with bones well-covered. A "pot-bellied" puppy is not necessarily sufficiently fat. Quite the reverse is sometimes the case, for a distended abdomen can be caused by malnutrition, worms or other troubles. An accepted method of testing for proper plumpness is to feel for the top of the pelvic bone on the back in front of the tail's base. The area should be well-rounded and firm, with bones scarcely perceptible. Excessively knobby knees may mean rickets induced by insufficient calcium intake.

If there is any question in your mind about the health of the puppy you have set your heart on buying, the breeder should be glad to have it checked by a veterinarian, and to give you the vet's written opinion of the dog's condition. Though you may be reluctant to eliminate from consideration a puppy whose sound health is not medically certified, it can be better in the end.

Temperament

At any age, the typical Keeshond is friendly and not afraid of anything or anybody. The varying degrees of those characteristics depend on a puppy's genealogical background and its own contact with people. To see either or both of a litter's parents can give you helpful clues as to how the particular puppies may develop in regard to temperament and other attributes. But don't be shocked by the dam's appearance. By the time you see her she will have probably lost her coat, due to pregnancy and nursing her brood, and you may therefore only be able to judge her structure and disposition.

A Keeshond puppy which piddles when you pet or pick it up is a rarity, and indicates unnatural nervousness, which it may or may not outgrow. If you clap your hands loudly, most little Kees will merely look up at you in surprise. Any that cringe or scuttle away are not typical, although this may be caused by previous lack of exposure to noise. But which of the litter will turn out to be the best and most devoted as *your* dog, is anyone's guess. The main thing is to decide which puppy you find most appealing.

Selecting Breeding and/or Show Prospects

Whenever puppies are to be selected for breeding and/or show, thorough study of the Standard is a must. It is also valuable to have a knowledge of genetics and of the individual Keeshonden in the pedigree of puppies you are considering. The good points and faults in every dog are inherited from its parents and their ancestors, and in turn, are transmittable to its descendants. Learning about a litter's forebears takes a bit of doing, but is well worth the effort. Photographs and show records can help. And while it is true that champions may range in quality from excellent to poor, dependent upon the competition they encountered and the number of times they were shown, a championship title does indicate some degree of recognized merit.

Another important aid to prospective breeders and exhibitors is to watch Keeshond judging at shows. This gives you the opportunity to compare a number of Kees together in the ring, and to gain an awareness of the various degrees of quality in the breed. Read books on dog breeding and showing (see Appendix). Ask successful breeders for advice, and study pictures of winning Keeshonden published in the dog magazines. Then give yourself a chance to absorb all the information you have acquired. The longer you raise dogs, the more you will find that there is always more to be learned.

Structure and Gait

At eight weeks old, the structure of the Keeshond is usually a miniature version of an adult. It should have a short back, sloping slightly from the top of the shoulders (at the withers) to the hips. A back which slopes toward the head is a fault and is not likely to improve with age. The rib cage should be well-rounded, not "slab sided", and there should be good depth of chest and width between the front legs. All legs should have plenty of bone without coarseness.

Although some allowance can be made for the floppiness of youth, soundness of gait and stance are essential in Kees of all ages. (For detailed discussion of soundness, see chapter 7). To check a puppy's action and stance, watch how it trots to its breeder, and back to you when called, and note how it stands naturally when it is at attention. Remember, even a poor specimen can be made to look like a world-beater if it is "set up" on the floor or a table by someone who knows how to manually place the dog's legs, tail and head for best effect. Frolicking little puppies are difficult to evaluate, but a well-constructed dog of any age should be able to set *itself* up properly.

Tail

To form the correct silhouette of the dog, at eight weeks old the base of the tail must be set well forward from the pelvic bone's rear protuberances (points of the "rump") and lie close to the back. Placement of the tail's base is easily found by placing your thumb and second finger on those points. Puppies' floppy tails can tighten up with age, but after eight weeks of age, a Keeshond's tail should never curve upwards from its base, or appear to be an appendage. It should always be part of the dog's outline.

Face, Eyes and Ears

Proper face markings, eyes, the size of ears and their placement, are all essential features of an adult Keeshond's typical head, and are

161

discernible in 8- to 12-week-old youngsters. A potentially good puppy has a black muzzle. If there is an intermixture of gray, or worst of all, tawny hair with the black, the muzzle will undoubtedly later become incorrectly light-colored or "streaky". The necessary light gray areas around the eyes and dark lines forming the required "spectacle" markings should always be present. It has been my experience that when the overall color of the hair on the top of a puppy's head is predominantly dark, all the correct face markings are more likely to be retained as an adult.

Eye color, shape and placement are important. Oval, very dark brown eyes are required, the darker the better, and light eyes are a definite fault. It is quite easy to recognize eyes that are not oval, that bulge, or are placed too far apart or too close. But to judge what color a puppy's eyes may be at maturity is something else again. All Kees puppies' eyes seem dark at first glance. But don't be misled by this. Look at them closely with a good light on their beguiling faces. Their eyes are actually dark *blue* when very young. The depth of blue throughout the eye is a clue as to what shade of brown the eyes may be in future. Whenever youngsters' eyes are not deep, dark blue, or when a lighter band of color is perceptible around the perimeter of the eye—beware!

Ears should be small, triangular in shape, mounted high on the head, carried erect and covered with velvety black hair. Very big or wide-set ears in a puppy are faults which should be definitely avoided when choosing a show prospect. At eight weeks old, it is often a problem to judge ears because they have usually just started to come up, and some are not up at all. I have found that a helpful way to check ear placement and size in proportion to the head is to lay the puppy on its back, so that the ears fall back into somewhat the position they may have later. At 12 to 16 weeks, all ears should be up. In exceptionally heavy-coated litters, it is advisable to trim off the fur on the back of the tips of the ears, to expedite having the ears stand up straight. While the Kees is teething, at about five months of age, its ears sometimes droop temporarily. But a grown Keeshond's ears should *never* fold forward, have a "poke-bonnet" effect, or point away from each other like a bat's.

Orchidism

In most 8-to-12-week-old male Kees, both testicles can be found in, or right near, the scrotum. If that is not the case, you would be well advised to inquire about the litter's sire and other male forebears' development in this respect. There occasionally are Kees dogs that mature more slowly than normal, but by six months of age, at the latest, a Keeshond should be a complete male in every way. An adult dog of any breed whose testicles are not both in the scrotum is a "monorchid" or "cryptorchid" and is disqualified in the show ring. (In dog parlance, *cryptorchid* identifies the bilateral cryptorchid, whose testicles are both abnormally retained in the abdominal cavity, and have not descended into the scrotum; *monorchid* identifies the unilateral cryptorchid, with one testicle retained and one descended into the scrotum.) Authorities point out that when congenital, these physical defects are considered inheritable.

Head

The younger the puppy, the more difficult it is to estimate what its head will be like as an adult. Very young puppies' heads are apt to seem too big for their bodies, but the skull should be wedge-shaped and somewhat flat, not "domey", and must have a definite indentation—or "stop" as it is called—between the eyes. Be sure the jaws meet in front in a "scissors bite" with the upper teeth just overlapping those on the lower jaw. An "undershot" or "overshot" mouth is an inheritable fault, but is fortunately seldom found in the Keeshond.

Coat Texture, Color and Markings

Puppies' coats should be dense, with a thick, downy undercoat and coarse guard hairs. When you run your hand over them toward the head, the fur should show a very light gray or very pale cream undercoat beneath black-tipped outer hairs, and feel slightly harsh. Baby bitches' fur is sometimes softer than dogs', and the texture of the new coats grown by matrons after whelping is nearly always quite soft at first, but should harshen up later.

In 8-to-10-weekolders, the overall coloring and markings called for in the standard should be well indicated. The relatively minor faults of "smutty" colored, darkish legs, black "thumb marks" below the knees, black toe markings, very small white patches on chest and feet, and creaminess around the ears, often—but not always—clear up. It is most important that the coloring of the puppies be of shades of lightest gray or almost-white cream through medium gray to black. The general effect in the whole dog can legitimately vary from light to dark. But tawniness in areas which should be light gray and/or a brown cast in the hair wherever black tipping should be present, are serious faults. The Standard states: "any pronounced deviation from the gray color is not permissible".

Your New Puppy

Let us think about how and when to introduce a puppy into a new home so that the best results are achieved on all counts.

It may seem to be a jolly idea to give a dog to children for Christmas, jolly perhaps for the youngsters. But what about the puppy? Christmas, the most tumultuous season of the year is the worst possible time for a dog to adjust to a new life. He has left the only home and security he has ever known. He has been subjected to the terrors and hazards of plane or rail shipment when traffic is the heaviest. He finds himself in a strange world filled with strangers. To add to his unhappiness, his new owners may hide him away somewhere, so his lonely weeping for his lost home will not divulge his presence before "Santa Clause comes".

When the great day arrives, the bewildered, helpless little dog— probably with a big red bow tied around his neck—is put under the Christmas tree in a mass of toys, surrounded by squealing children and googling adults.

The fact that he is frightened and miserable can be lost sight of on such a day by old and young alike, and he is treated like just another inanimate toy. For hours he may be yanked back and forth with shouts of "He's mine!" Or he is hauled around by a string or his tail, or squeezed.

Finally, either because the feeding and house training schedules supplied by the puppy's breeder have been ignored, or due to the nerve-wracking treatment he has received, or both—the puppy makes a puddle on the living room carpet. Come cries of "dirty dog" from unthinking adults and sometimes he is even punished for what was really caused by his new owners' thoughtlessness.

The Right Start

Long before a puppy's arrival, children and their parents need to realize the importance of treating the small newcomer gently, with due emphasis on consideration for *his* feelings, his need for regularly scheduled meals, trips outdoors for house-training, lots of daytime sleep and a bed or place of his own in the house.

The best way to give your puppy the help he needs in adjusting to his new home is to plan his arrival when it is most convenient and practical for you to give him the special care and attention necessary for the first few weeks at least. For instance, while children are at school, their mother has more time to give to a puppy and he can then have the daily rest he requires for sturdy growth. A question to decide is at what time of year do weather conditions in your area make it easiest to house train a dog. Another pertinent point to consider is that rail and plane transportation are nightmarish episodes for shipper and dogs, which too often result in anguish and even death for animals, particularly during holiday rush periods.

All this indicates that it is far better to bring a puppy into your home at almost any time other than during major holidays. So whenever it seems appropriate to you, why not announce long in advance that a puppy will join the family at some future date? It will build an anticipation of that happy event. An understanding of what it means for the dog as well as what it means to them, can be a joyful and character-building experience for your young people. Spreading the delivery of puppies throughout the year is also advantageous to breeders as well as to puppies.

After all, of what lasting value to anyone are a few extra, childish shrieks of surprise on finding a puppy with the Christmas toys or Easter eggs? With the true spirit of Christmas and Easter in our hearts all year around, let us always try to bring about more understanding and kindness for dogs and all animals.

Puppies at four weeks.

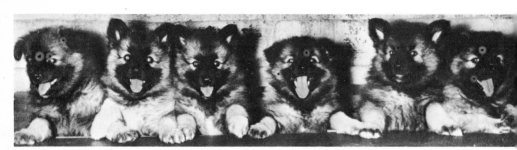

Six weeks.

Ten weeks.

166

Stages of Development

At birth, Kees weigh about 9 to 12 ounces, and look like small, very dark rats, with heads that are proportionately too large, and long, straight tails. But cheer up . . .

By the second day, their coats have fluffed out, some markings may appear, and they begin to look like Keeshonden. From then on, the rate of growth is astounding.

In ten days, eyes start to open. A bit later, teeth poke through the gums, and tails turn toward the head.

At six weeks some ears begin to come up, and from here to 12 weeks is a glamorous age. In fact, Kees puppies are then so enchanting they seem like unbelievably beautiful silver-gray-to-black-shaded teddy bears. It has seemed to me that the puppies whose ears are the first to stand upright are apt to be smaller dogs than the others in that litter at maturity.

At about 16 weeks, the second teething starts, and from that age until six months, many Kees go through a gawky, adolescent stage, through which they look awful and rather comical. They seem to be all legs and ears, and to have a strangely colored and too-short coat in relation to their size. The undercoat may have become a rather dark cream color, and have grown out over the guard hairs so that the whole dog appears to be light tan, except for the gray and black face markings and dark ears.

However, by the time the first adult coat develops at from six to eight months, it should have all the required, typical, gray-to-black shadings and markings.

Some puppies develop faster than others, and those which mature slowly may turn out to be the best at two to three years of age, when the average Keeshond is in full bloom.

Ten weeks.

Four-and-a-half months.

Eight months.

What to Require of the Breeder

All breeders should give buyers of their dogs the following *written* information:

* Details of the dog's diet and feeding schedule.
  (A sudden change in the amount and kind of food can cause diarrhea).
* Data on all wormings, and the inoculations given against distemper, hepatitis, leptospirosis, etc. prior to delivery to the purchaser.
* The Keeshond's four-generation pedigree.
* With any dog represented as purebred, Chapter 3, Section 5, of the American Kennel Club Rules and Regulations, requires that the seller must complete and deliver to the buyer the AKC's official forms necessary for registering the dog—unless otherwise agreed to by the seller and buyer in written, signed statements.
* A bill of sale.
* A veterinarian's health certificate.
* A copy of the veterinarian's statement of his findings re X-rays of both of the dog's parents in respect to any potentially inheritable bone malformation such as hip dysplasia.

As a practical, routine procedure for the benefit of everyone concerned, all financial and other arrangements between the seller and buyer should always be clearly defined in written agreements signed by both parties. This rule, of course, also applies for such transactions as stud services, or leasing dogs or bitches on breeding terms. No matter how honest and well-intentioned the people involved may be, verbal understandings can lead to unfortunate misunderstandings and consequent problems.

When you buy your first Keeshond, you may think you will never raise a litter, use your dog at stud, or enter dog shows. But as time goes on, you may change your mind. Many owners do. So for every reason, get the best puppy possible!

169

Two days old.

9

Breeding the Keeshond

WHEN a Keeshond first joins your family you may firmly believe you will never have a litter of your own. But do not be surprised when your and your friends' enthusiasm for the lovable female in your home make you eager to have puppies. In fact the breed's history shows that the greatest number of Keeshond breeders started out as pet owners. And it should be noted that many of them also learned the hard way that breeding dogs is not something to be undertaken lightly or inadvisedly.

To raise Kees puppies can be a great and happy experience. But there is far more involved than just having a boxful of from five to eight or more glamorous puppies to admire and play with in the house. "Operation PUPP" as I call it, is not all fun and games. It means picking-up-puppy-papers, feeding, weaning, worming, inoculations, pre-natal and post-natal care of the dam, whelping and so on. The whole project takes much time, knowledge and expense, all of which points up the need to learn everything possible on the subject before deciding to raise a litter.

The word *breeder* technically applies to the owner or lessee of the dam of a litter at the time the mating took place. But the owner of every male who sires a litter is equally responsible for the production of puppies and should apply controls accordingly. Dogs of either sex which have improper temperament or are of poor quality should of course not be bred. Nor should owners of good quality dogs allow them to be used at stud by irresponsible breeders, nor to be mated to bitches which for any reason are unsuitable for breeding. Only thus can stud owners fulfill at least part of their obligations to their own and their dogs' reputations, the bitch owners and the breed.

Breeders' Responsibilities

When you stop to think about it, you realize that the puppies you decide to raise come into existence only because you choose to produce them. Those little dogs are therefore *your* responsibility from the time you planned the litter and mated the parents. They depend wholly on you to help safeguard their welfare to the best of your ability in every way. And this requires that you personally select proper homes for those you sell—an undertaking that is not always as easy as might be expected.

Many other breeds are far better known throughout the country than the Keeshond and are consequently in greater demand. That is one reason why conscientious Keeshond breeders who have their puppies' interests at heart, limit their production in relation to the potential opportunities to properly place Kees in their particular area.

Every breeder of even one litter also has a responsibility to the breed as a whole. Whether the effects are good or bad depends to a great extent on the quality of the puppies and the breeders' understanding of ethical breeding practices and of their responsibility to make every effort to carry out those practices. The Keeshond Club of America's Breeders' Code of Ethics (p. 178) provides basic information on this vital subject.

Planning a Litter

It is to the obvious benefit of everyone who plans a litter for the first or the umpteenth time to aim for the best possible results. This requires using only the best bitches and studs you can find and afford. Remember also, that as mentioned in Chapter 8, it takes no more work or expense to raise potentially good dogs than others.

For a reasonable expectation of desirable results, careful selection of both parents for a litter is a must. Decisions as to whether or not particular dogs and bitches should be mated *to each other,* or used for breeding at all, should be based on thorough study of the Standard (p. 141), the pictorially presented *Keeshond Rights and Wrongs* (pp. 147–149) and acquisition of as much information as possible about the attributes of Kees in the specific pedigrees. Though it is often difficult to be unswayed by our affection for our own dogs, unemotional evaluation of the good points and *faults* in the bitches and studs under consideration is absolutely essential.

Importance of Genetic Knowledge

When breeding dogs we are dealing with nature's hereditary laws. The findings of experienced breeders and authorities on genetics indicate that to attempt to produce worthwhile dogs without at least a basic knowledge and application of those laws is like fishing with a bare hook. By sheer luck, a good specimen may be snagged out of the ancestral ocean, but the chances are mighty slim.

For more than a century, scientific research has been devoted to the branch of biology that deals with heredity and is known as *genetics.* The apparent conclusions reached by geneticists are that *only line breeding* and/or *inbreeding,* combined with judicious *outbreeding* when advisable, can if properly used, genetically "fix" as inheritable *dominants* the *chromosomes* and *genes* which transmit correct type and temperament to subsequent generations of animals.

For the same reasons however, close breeding also fixes *faults* as well as good points, and can bring out in the offspring, either good or bad attributes carried as *recessives* by both parents. Therefore to line breed mediocre or worse members of a breed, or to mate any which have the same obvious, major faults, would be unwise to say the least.

Outbreeding can be a constructive factor at times. But haphazard or continuous outbreeding accomplishes little or nothing of enduring value for breeders or the breed as it does not establish an actual line.

173

The whole subject is exceedingly interesting and important. Fortunately excellent books have been written on genetics in relation to dog breeding. One I recommend highly is *The New Art of Breeding Better Dogs* by Kyle and Philip Onstott, published by Howell Book House.

Breeding for Correct Color

The approved coloration of the Keeshond in the United States is clearly described in our Standard as: "A mixture of gray and black. The undercoat should be very pale gray or cream (not tawny) ." But what do we often find in the show rings? An incorrect mish-mash of coloration composed of gray, tawniness and even dark, reddish brown. Muzzles are sometimes far from being dark and are brownish or streaked with tan or gray. In varying degrees, the undercoat is tawny, particularly around the ears, and where black tipping is called for, the hair may be rusty brown. The whole effect is a far cry from the appearance of elegance presented by Keeshonden whose color and markings are in accordance with our Standard. And that document is explicit on the subject. Why then does the breed continue to have this problem? There are a number of possible reasons.

In addition to the pale-gray-to-black coloration recognized by the British and American Kennel Clubs, all white, all black and entirely pale-orange-to-liver colored Kees without a gray, white or black hair on them, have been accepted in Holland and Germany for years. Presumably the gray and the orange Kees have been crossbred at one time or another and subsequent breeders have not had sufficient genetic information combined with a desire to breed selectively in regard to color. If selective breeding had been generally practiced in this respect, mixed up coloring would not still exist.

If not entirely bred out of a line, the microscopic genes for orange-to-liver coat color tenaciously carry out genetic laws. As cases in point, one or more completely orange-to-liver colored Keeshond puppies are occasionally produced by gray-to-black parents in the same litter with other correctly gray-to-black members. In such instances the litter's parents must have carried the recessive genes for orange-liver pigmentation from their ancestors, and the specific mating combined those off-beat genes to produce the orange type offspring.

The same thing is known to occur in Norwegian Elkhounds. In

fact the author saw a completely orange-to-liver shaded Elkhound puppy benched for *exhibition only* at one of the famous Morris and Essex Kennel Club shows in New Jersey years ago.

Although the few orange Kees I have seen were very beautiful, they should never be registered or bred, nor should there be a repeat breeding of their parents. In my opinion however, anyone who destroys a healthy, gentle dog is the merciless murderer of a helpless animal which is fully entitled to its life as someone's pet.

When some Kees are shedding, their fur loses pigmentation to some extent. It becomes temporarily drab and faded, sometimes to the point of being slightly brown and tawny where normally black and clear gray. It is said that sunburn also affects coat color. The average Keeshond however, is not a sun-bather at any time of the year if shade is available, and unless a dog lies on its back in the sun for a considerable time, the hair on its underside, or under the jaw and on the chest would not be affected by the sun. So, to see what the color situation is in those particular areas on a Keeshond when it is not shedding and is said to be sunburned, just turn the dog on its back, examine the fur in a good light and draw your own conclusions.

Questions to Buyers

As an aid to evaluation of people's qualifications as dog owners, the author has found it exceedingly helpful as routine procedure, to ask specific questions of everyone who wants to buy a Keeshond for whatever purpose. I prefer to ask them personally rather than by letter. One can learn so much about a person's attitude toward animals when talking to them, that it is well worth the cost of a telephone call.

The following are some of my queries to pet buyers. "Why do you want a dog, particularly a Keeshond?" "Do all the adults in your family want a dog?" "Who will take care of it?" "Where will it sleep?" "Will the puppy be left alone all day?" "Have you, or do you plan to have an outdoor enclosure for a dog?"

If a female is desired, I add: "Do you expect to raise a litter?" "Are you prepared to spend the necessary amount of time, work and money?" "How will you find good homes for the puppies you sell?" And I always point out the advantages and urge the spaying of bitches which are not to be bred.

My questions to people who are interested in stud service or breeding stock include: "What is your purpose in raising Keeshonden?" "Have you a copy of the Standard and the Breeders' Code of Ethics?" "Do you show or plan to show your dogs?" "How do you plan to sell puppies?" "Have you raised, or are you now raising other breeds, if so, what breeds?" "Have the hips of the Kees you own been X-rayed and pronounced normal?" "Please send me the pedigree of the bitch for whom you want stud service."

The reason for some of those questions may seem somewhat obscure at first glance, but experience has proved them valuable in many ways. For example, a Mrs. X wrote me that she wanted a male to breed to her three adult bitches and to a puppy bitch from one of two previous litters. There was no other information except that she and her husband lived on a farm in the Midwest. Her answers to my questions revealed the following: Mrs. X was raising ten breeds, ranging in size from Pekingese to Boxers "as a pastime and added revenue". She planned "to establish a market for Keeshonds through dealers that handle these dogs." She did not have the Keeshond Standard or show her dogs. In other words, a typical puppy mill. All Mrs. X received from me was my opinion of that type of operation and a copy of the Keeshond Club of America's Breeders' Code of Ethics.

Temperament

The deterioration of the originally sound temperament of many other breeds has been caused by the deliberate mating of dogs of questionable or improper dispositions by people who apparently did not realize or care what they were doing to damage their own and their breed's reputations.

The Keeshond, however, has been fortunate in this respect so far. Breeders have apparently been mindful of the importance of only using for breeding, dogs and bitches which have inherited the breed's typical gentle nature. Nevertheless, *right temperament above all* should always be the watchword of every Keeshond breeder.

Right Type

In *Blueprint of the Keeshond* we discussed the two somewhat different types in the breed, the reasons they exist today and the fact that the American Standard states: "When dogs are judged equal in type, the dog nearest the ideal height is to be preferred." It also says, "size consideration should not outweigh that of type." So, whenever a breeding program or even one litter is being planned, breeders would be well advised to studiously consider the differences between the two types and always aim to produce the Keeshond described in the Standard.

Improvement

Show records are significant evidence of the steady rise in the over-all quality of Keeshonden in the United States and other areas, especially in recent years. As a breeder, exhibitor and judge, the author has had the opportunity and pleasure of seeing at first hand, the increasing excellence of Kees in the rings in different parts of this country.

Hearty congratulations to all those who have accomplished so much. This does not mean, however, that breeders can relax their efforts in future. There are still many points which warrant improvement and serious consideration when making breeding plans, namely: better top-line, eye and coat color, legs and gait, and placement and length of neck. The higher your goals are set, the better.

The future of the Keeshond is in the hands of every breeder of every litter, a big responsibility.

Code of Ethics
for breeders and owners of Keeshonden

(Adopted by the Keeshond Club of America)

This Code of Ethics is presented as an informative guide for breeders and potential breeders of Keeshonden, whose foremost aims are the welfare and improvement of the breed. The By-Laws of The Keeshond Club of America state that the club "shall do all in its power to protect and advance the interests of the breed". In applying for membership, applicants agree to further the club's objectives, and to conduct all their activities in connection with the breed in accordance with the Club's Breeder's Code of Ethics.

An ethical breeder conducts his activities as follows:

Breeding:

He conscientiously plans each litter based on the parents' appropriate temperament and qualities in relation to the breed's official Standard, and before deciding to produce a litter, considers the possibilities of properly placing puppies he cannot keep himself.

He only uses for breeding, adults which are of sound temperament, which are free from congenital defects such as hereditary orchidism (i.e., males whose testicles are not both normally descended), blindness, deafness, etc., and whose hips have been X-rayed with proper positioning and pronounced normal by a veterinarian personally qualified in the field of hip-dysplasia.

He only breeds healthy, mature bitches (preferably after one year of age and after the first season), and allows proper spacing between litters. He urges bitch purchasers to spay those which for any reason will not be used for breeding, and to properly safeguard unspayed bitches from unplanned matings.

Health:

All of his stock is kept under sanitary conditions and is given maximum health protection through worming and inoculations.

Registration:

He registers his breeding stock with the American Kennel Club, and keeps accurate records of matings and pedigrees.

Sales:

He does not sell or consign puppies or adults to pet shops or other commercial dealers.

He sells Keeshonden, permits stud service, and leases studs or bitches ONLY to individuals who give satisfactory evidence that they will give them proper care and attention, and are in accord with this Code of Ethics. He Makes available to the novice the benefit of his advice and experience. All stock leaving his possession is at least 8 weeks old. He provides buyers with written details on feeding; general care; data on worming and innoculations against distemper, hepatitis, leptospirosis, etc., and the Keeshond's 4-generation pedigree. He provides and requires written agreements signed by all parties to all sales and other transactions, and accordingly completes and delivers the forms necessary for registration. (NOTE: Under American Kennel Club rules [Chapter 3, Section 6] ALL such forms MUST BE COMPLETED AND SUPPLIED by all parties to transactions, unless they have agreed otherwise in *written, signed* agreements.)

All his advertising is factual. It does not offer Keeshonden at less than the minimum price, nor is it so worded as to attract undesirable buyers, or to encourage raising Keeshonden merely as a money-making scheme.

He does not supply Keeshonden for raffles, "give-away" prizes or other such projects.

Price:

By setting a minimum price for his young puppies of at least $75. to $125. (dependent on geographic location), he upholds the value of the breed and of his own stock. He gives his adults and puppies first class care and cannot afford to sell at a low price.

Conduct:

When confronted by a situation not covered by this Code of Ethics, he conducts himself as he would like to be treated under similar circumstances.

10

Care of the Keeshond

KEESHONDEN are inherently sturdy, healthy dogs, and at any age, readily adapt themselves to new owners and surroundings. This does not mean, however, that the Keeshond is a dog to be left alone outdoors at all times, or relegated to living only in a kennel. Far from it. Kees are instinctively house-dogs and so affectionate that it is exceedingly important for them to be closely associated with their owners in the home. Because of this characteristic, owners who find it necessary to house a number of their Kees in a kennel, bring two or more of the dogs into their homes each day to take turns as house-pets on a rotating basis.

Runs and Shade

The grim menace of death-dealing cars, the vile "dog-nappers" who steal pets to sell them for laboratory research, and all the other hazards which threaten all loose running dogs, make it essential to provide some type of outdoor enclosure as a protection for pets. A wire run, close to, or attached to the home is a safeguard for the dog and a convenience for owners, and need not be costly. Heavy gauge chicken wire, and the metal posts that go with it, will do.

Another type of do-it-yourself run is portable. It consists of panels and gates made of chain-link fencing attached to galvanized metal tubing, and is available through building supply companies, hardware stores, or direct from manufacturers. The panels come in various lengths and heights, are rigid, require no posts, and can be easily and quickly put together on level ground by any two people who can handle a pair of pliers, a bolt and a nut.

For the welfare and comfort of Kees, shade should always be available to them. Wherever natural shade is lacking, the slatted snow-fencing sold at lumber yards is an economical answer to the problem. A slat roof can be formed over the above type of panelled runs as follows: Place two or more 2x4s across the top of the run and wire them to the top of the fence panels. Then on top of the 2x4s lay two alternating layers of snow fencing, so that the slats of the top layer cover the spaces between the slats on the bottom strip, and wire both strips down where needed. This simple type of shade roof also allows the air circulation needed in hot weather, whereas under Fiberglas roofing, for example, the heat is trapped and creates an intolerable temperature for the dogs.

Grooming

The Keeshond is easy to maintain in good condition because the composition and texture of the coat are a deterrent to insects and most dirt can be readily brushed off. Professional trimming or grooming are unnecessary. The coat seldom mats, unless burrs or such are involved, and the breed does not have any "doggy" odor. A bath is therefore rarely needed. (Because bathing softens the coat, if it is deemed necessary to bathe a show Keeshond, it should be done at least a week before exhibiting.) As a rule, a light sponging with half-and-half rubbing alcohol and water, combined with brushing, are adequate to remove dust and fluff out the fur.

However, the Keeshond should be brushed regularly, about every two weeks, to ensure a more comfortable and beautiful pet. For convenience in all grooming, place the dog on a table, laying him gently first on one side, and then the other. It is a good idea to start this procedure when puppies are about 12 weeks old. They quickly learn the routine, and if care is taken not to hurt them, enjoy it. A long-bristled, wire brush of the "roll" type is generally used. All brushing should be from the skin out, done in small sections at a time and *always toward the head*. In fact, when patting Kees, the fur should be rubbed forward to keep it from standing out from the body.

Where the coat is particularly dense and long, as in the ruff, fore-leg feathering, tail and britches, it is advisable to follow up after brushing these areas with use of a wide-toothed metal dog comb, which easily removes any remaining loose fur.

Free air circulation to the skin is important at all times to maintain normal skin condition, especially during once-a-year shedding, and in hot or humid weather. But Kees should *never* be shaved. To remove the dog's coat, which is its natural protection against heat and cold, can cause great discomfort and even be harmful to health.

Whenever bathing seems desirable, only a good dog soap or shampoo should be used. *Never* use detergents of any kind. They can dry up the needed natural oil in the skin and cause a dandruff condition which may lead to eczema. Before bathing, be sure to brush thoroughly to get out all the loose fur. Otherwise, the dog will come out of the water looking like a lumpy quilt, and the remaining tufts of undercoat are then less easily removed. Put cotton in the dog's ears, protect its eyes from soap suds, and make sure the coat is thoroughly rinsed. Before the dog is allowed outdoors or in drafty quarters, he should be completely dry. To speed up the drying process after toweling, a hair dryer used in conjunction with brushing is helpful.

Dogs' nails and feet also deserve regular attention. To prevent flat-footedness and "going back on pasterns", nails should be frequently clipped with dog nail-clippers and then filed back as far as possible without getting into the quick. Or if owners are timid about nail-clippers, just filing with the large, coarse wood files sold in hardware stores can be sufficient.

Before shows: with curved, blunt-end little scissors, round off the hair on feet to show their cat-like shape, and cut off fur growing beyond the pads. With straight scissors, trim evenly any ragged fur on the back of the hind legs from the foot up to the leg joint (hock). For added glamour in the rings, many exhibitors use commercial coat sprays before brushing (none which are yellow should be used on Kees), and some people trim off the whiskers on muzzles. Finally, brush up the ruff in a flare. Spread the britches to look like "pantaloons" and, holding the tail by its tip, fan the plume forward with the brush. With one shake your Keeshond is a handsome picture as he steps into the ring with every hair in place. But in the ring or out, wherever you and your Keeshond are seen, grooming can enhance his natural beauty so that he attracts admiring attention, and is a source of pride for his owner.

Feeding

The Keeshond is a notoriously eager eater, but like any other dog, can become spoiled in that respect by well-meaning owners.

To maintain good eating habits and health, puppies and grown dogs should only be given proper sized, balanced meals, and never be coaxed to eat, or scolded if they don't. Just remove all food not gobbled up after a few minutes, and feed *nothing* until the next scheduled feeding time. This is emotionally hard on owners but usually brings the desired result. Food left for dogs of any age to pick at whenever it strikes their fancy to do so, or tidbits given between meals, can turn otherwise good eaters into either finicky or overweight animals, or both. However, if a dog's appetite continues to fall off, or if he refuses to eat for no apparent reason, a veterinarian should be promptly consulted.

Feeding at set hours is best for dogs and helpful to owners. The fact that a dog's consumption of his food is shortly followed by bowel elimination, contributes to easier house training and cleaning runs at regular times.

The notion that bones are good for dogs is far from correct. Though it may be fun for them, and help remove tartar from the teeth, to gnaw on bones is actually dangerous. Countless dogs die every year from the results of vital organs being pierced by bone splinters. Pet supply stores offer a variety of safe substitutes to chew on, but if you feel you must give your dog the real thing, *only* let him have the middle section of a beef shin bone, sawed straight across.

We often hear people say that their dog is as well fed as they are because he gets the leftovers from their meals. Table scraps may be tasty, but do not provide enough daily, balanced nourishment for dogs. On the other hand, the available commercial dog foods and additives are based on years of professional research on canine nutrition.

Marie Wilson and Groucho Marx feed Ch. Haarl van Fitz at California sanction match.

The number of different, successful diets for feeding grown dogs and raising puppies can be bewildering, especially to new owners and breeders. We can only try to learn as much as possible on the subject, and adopt what seems the most effective for our own dogs. The author has found the following program satisfactory:

Regular Diet for Adults

The adults have one meal a day, fed in the morning. It consists of dog kibble, slightly softened in water, canned beef or horsemeat, powdered vitamins, brewer's yeast powder, cod liver oil and corn oil, plus a large dog biscuit for "dessert" and to help keep teeth clean. Quantities of each ingredient should be governed by your veterinarian's advice and varying degrees of assimilation in specific dogs.

Diet for Nursing Bitches

Four weeks after mating, the bitch starts having a second daily

185

meal of about half the size of the first, with calcium phosphate dibasic powder added to the other ingredients at the fifth week. The second feeding is necessary to supply enough nutrition and calcium for the puppies and dam. Her supplementary meal is gradually increased to a full meal, and a dish of half-and-half evaporated canned milk and water is given to her at noon. Again, professional advice is advisable, for over-feeding as well as under-feeding is to be avoided.

While nursing, the dam is given three medium-sized daily meals with powdered calcium in each and, unless she produces too much milk, she is given all the milk and water mixture she will drink in between. Calcium intake is vital for mother and puppies. If at any time the bitch gets a staring expression, and pants excessively, it can be a sympton of eclampsia, caused by calcium deficiency, which can be fatal to her, and calls for a veterinarian on the run.

Feeding Puppies

It is important that all puppies have an equal chance to nurse. Litters of eight or more should at first be divided into two groups— one group left with the dam while the other is in a box slightly warmed by a heating pad under a thick towel. Then, every two hours, comes the "changing of the guard", which is continued as long as seems necessary. This is no picnic for the breeder, but can make the difference between success or failure in raising the whole litter as sturdy youngsters.

In spite of the essential worming of the bitch before mating, most litters have roundworms and when about three weeks old, a bowel sample should be checked by a veterinarian. And don't wait until the infestation is so bad that worms turn up in the pen! Fortunately, veterinarians can supply roundworm medication which does not require starving the puppies or coping with loose bowels, and which can be given at home.

At three weeks or less, the puppies are started on half-and-half evaporated milk and HOT water, or canned puppy formula as directed, combined with human baby cereal once a day. A few days later a second daily meal is added, consisting of warmed, finely ground, lean raw beef with a pinch of calcium in a tiny meat ball, fed by hand at first, followed by a drop of liquid vitamins on the tongue. To ensure even amounts of food for all, when puppies are first eating on their own, muffin tins are useful. And when older,

186

large ring molds help keep puppies from diving bodily into their chow.

The number of meals and amounts gradually increase to five daily during and after weaning, with puppy meal and canned beef or horsemeat substituted for baby cereal and raw beef. At six weeks, the litter is completely weaned. By ten weeks they are on four meals, two of milk and meal, and two of meat, meal, cod liver oil, powdered vitamins, calcium, brewer's yeast, corn oil, and a small biscuit. At six months, they have only the two meals of the meat and meal mixture. After one year old, they are on the one daily meal for adult dogs, and calcium is omitted except for females in whelp.

Good nourishment, and lots of TLC (tender, loving care) are all that is needed to keep Keeshonden healthy, happy and handsome.

Mrs. Kenneth Fitzpatrick with "sled" team of Keeshonden in California.

11

Leash Training

KEESHONDEN are quick and eager to learn, and they remember their experiences. This makes it very important that their "lessons" be happy experiences for them and that good habits are formed right from the start. All training can accomplish this, if owners always keep in mind how they themselves would react to the teaching method *if they were the dog*.

Applying this to leash training, how would we feel if something strange was put around our neck and we were chokingly yanked along on a lead, especially if *any* type of choke collar was used? Wouldn't we be frightened and miserable, and do our best to get away from it all—but fast? And dogs do just that. Thus the bad habit of pulling on a lead might get its start.

Only a few, brief sessions are needed for leash training if owners make it fun for the dog and follow a routine. Long before any training, a puppy should become completely accustomed to wearing a collar—the lightest weight, rounded leather one obtainable. This type is also recommended for Kees of all ages at all times because they do not need heavy collars and straight-edged ones and choke chains wear down their ruffs.

It is best to start lessons in an enclosed area such as a screened porch, garage or living room. Thus, there are no outdoor distractions such as squirrels, or blowing leaves. With puppy on your left side, and small bits of food in your right hand held above his head, walk counter-clockwise around the enclosure *without* a leash, quietly saying "heel" and giving him crumbs and praise for following along. In no time he will be happily pattering along beside your left knee and enjoying it.

After a few such sessions of about 15 minutes each, attach a short bantam-weight leash to his collar and proceed as before. A braided, plastic leash is useful and can be held in your left hand. Chances are the dog won't even notice the lead because he is enjoying the tidbits and walking with you. During this stage of training if for any reason he starts to go away from you, by all means go with him, so he will not feel any frightening pressure on his neck to make him struggle against a taut lead. Very soon, puppy will be ready to go on an outdoor walk or into the show ring, trotting at your side on a completely loose lead.

However, if at any time thereafter he starts to move ahead of you or pull on the leash, give it a quick, sharp jerk backwards (not up), say "Heel!" and instantly loosen it again. It is the quickness of the jerk and return to a loose lead which is effective. If you just pull back or hold the leash taut, this can make the dog pull against it that much more, and he acquires the habit of literally *taking you* for a walk.

The Keeshond should be shown on a loose lead. To train a dog not to sniff the ground in the show ring, but to carry his head properly back on his shoulders, the author has found it most effective to always place the lead about two inches below the dog's jaw. A short lead in this position gives maximum control over the dog at all times.

Whenever you wish to give a dog a romp on a leash, it is best to do this on a very long cord (about 25 feet) while you stand still. This teaches him when to romp and when to trot properly at your side on a short, loose lead. We repeat, for all training, the best results come from trying to understandingly imagine one's self in the dog's place, and acting accordingly.

190

12

Showing Your Keeshond

THE underlying purpose of dog shows is to enable owners to receive the opinions of knowledgeable judges as to dogs' quality for breeding purposes. But shows offer more than that. In fact, to exhibit your pet in *Matches* and regular dog shows can open up a whole new world of pleasure and friendships—particularly if you never let your dogs' wins go to your head and you are a cheerful loser. Add to this, the ability to learn to recognize the good points in other people's dogs and the faults in your own, and you have a sound formula for deriving the greatest enjoyment from showing dogs. It should also be noted that judges' decisions are made in relation to the competition in the ring and the appearance of your dog on the particular day.

In case you have no idea of how to enter a dog, or of show procedure, here are some bits of information that may be useful.

As an aid to exhibitors, especially novices, local kennel clubs often hold ring handling classes and American Kennel Club *Sanctioned Matches,* both of which are open to the public and can be entered the day they are held. Match Shows are informal affairs where the ring and the judging procedures are similar to those at *regular* AKC, all-breed *point* shows and provide excellent training and experience for owners and dogs alike. Matches offer no points toward a championship title, but they are an economical and pleasant introduction to what goes on in the dog show world.

Point shows are those where championship points are awarded. To compete in them, all entries must be made several weeks ahead on the official entry forms available from the shows' Superintendents or The American Kennel Club, 51 Madison Ave., N.Y.C. 10010. To obtain the forms and/or the name and address of a nearby kennel club's Secretary (who can also give you the show Superintendents' address and the dates and location of shows scheduled to be held in your area), write to the AKC. Other possible sources of information about local kennel clubs and their activities are your town's officials, Chamber of Commerce and sports editors of local newspapers.

Championship Titles

To become a *champion of record,* the American Kennel Club requires that a dog or bitch must win a total of 15 points under at least three different judges, and those points must include a minimum of three in each of two shows (called "major" wins) under different judges.

Championship points are awarded to the *Winners Dog* (WD) and *Winners Bitch* (WB) —in other words, to the non-champion dog and bitch judged best in its breed in each show. The number of points acquired depends on the number of entries present over which the dog and bitch win their respective *Winners Class*—a class composed of the winners of each of the five classes for each sex, *Puppy, Novice, Bred by Exhibitor, American-Bred* and *Open.*

No more than five points can be won at any one show. The requirements for one through five-point wins vary in different breeds and geographical areas in the country. Those point schedules are annually established by the AKC and are printed in dog show catalogues.

On request, the AKC will send you a copy of its *Rules Applying to Registration and Dog Shows*—an important booklet to have on hand.

Best in Show Brace, Westminster 1962: Ch. Nederlan Herman v. Mack and litter brother, Ch. Nederlan Bruno v. Mack. Breeder: Mrs. J. Whitney Peterson. Owners: Mr. and Mrs. Emerson P. Hempstead.

Best in Show Brace, Westminster 1965: Ch. Von Storm's Prince Piet, bred by Nancy Riley, and sire Ch. Nederlan Herman v. Mack. Owners: Mr. and Mrs. Emerson P. Hempstead. (Judge, Haskell Schuffman. Handler, Roy Holloway.)

193

Equipment

The equipment needed at shows can be bought at pet supply shops or on show grounds. It consists of a show lead, long-bristled brush, metal comb, sponge or coat dressing spray, grooming table, and (for benched shows) a lightweight leather collar and bench chain. *Never* use a choke collar on the bench—it can strangle a dog. A wire crate is a necessity for unbenched shows, and very useful at benched events. Bring from home also, bits of cooked liver or other tidbits to keep your dog at attention in the ring, a plastic dish and a filled water bottle.

About a week before the show in which you have entered your pet, you will receive from the show's Superintendents an identification card with your entry's number, together with the judging program listing the ring number and time Kees will be judged and the time all dogs must be on the show grounds. Take these with you. Your entry's number is his bench number in the Keeshond section and is on the armband the ring steward gives you before you enter the ring.

At the Show

The breed's names are attached to the ends of benching rows. Other than that, you are usually on your own in finding your dog's bench. Except at a few shows, nobody ever seems to know where any breed is benched.

After your dog is settled on his bench or in his crate under tenting at outdoor, unbenched shows, locate the ring where Kees will be judged. All dogs should be at ringside when their class is called.

Never, *never* leave dogs in unattended vehicles at shows or anywhere else in warm weather. Even with automobile windows partly open, this practice has brought agony and death to countless, helpless dogs. And air-conditioning in cars cannot be depended upon. It often stops by itself and in addition, carbon monoxide seepage into a closed vehicle can be lethal.

In plenty of time before the Keeshond judging is scheduled, remove your dog's collar and put on the show lead. Slightly dampen his coat with a sponge or spray and brush thoroughly. In the ring, pay close attention to the judge's instructions. He will have the

Best in Show Brace, California 1946: Ch. Gungadin van Fitz and Ch. Clovelly Kris. Owners: Vera and Kenneth Fitzpatrick.

Best in Show Brace, Illinois 1969: Litter sisters, Ch. Gae-Kee Resplendent Aurora and Gae-Kee Addition to Westgate. Breeder-owners: Alice and Eugene Gamache.

Best in Show Brace, Boston: Ch. Nether-Lair's Damon de Gyselaer and son, Ch. Har-Curt's Hansel. Owner, Mrs. Harriet Ovington.

195

whole class trot around the ring counter-clockwise, line up at one side, stand for his inspection and individually trot away and back to him.

If your dog wins first or second in its class, be sure to stay at ringside to go back in again when his number is called for the Winners Class or possibly for Reserve Winners judging. The WD and WB compete with the champions present for *Best of Breed* (BOB) and *Best of Opposite Sex* to Best of Breed (BOS), and the *Best of Winners* (BOW) is chosen from between the WD and WB.

The BOB Keeshond later goes into the Non-Sporting Group ring in competition with the show's breed winners in Boston Terriers, Bulldogs, Chow Chows, Dalmations, French Bulldogs, Lhasa Apsos, Miniature and Standard Poodles and Schipperkes. The Group winner then contends for Best in Show (BIS) with the winners of the five other Groups—the Sporting breeds, Hounds, Working breeds, Terriers and Toys.

At the end of the day, win or lose, always remember that your dog is the same lovable, beautiful pet you left home with that morning. Nothing in the form of ribbons or lack of them can ever change that, any more than different judges' varying decisions can change the inherent qualities of any dog.

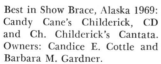

Best in Show Brace, Alaska 1969: Candy Cane's Childerick, CD and Ch. Childerick's Cantata. Owners: Candice E. Cottle and Barbara M. Gardner.

196

13

The Keeshond in Obedience

THE KEESHOND is known to be a happy, enthusiastic Obedience performer who is eager to work with and please his owners. In fact, the breed is often referred to as "a natural" in Obedience because of those particular characteristics. Despite a certain amount of disinterest in retrieving found in some members of the breed, the number of Keeshonden that have had perfect scores, Highest Scores in Trial and Highest Combined Scores, is impressive.

The first Keeshond in the world to earn a Companion Dog title (CD), completed it on the East Coast of the United States in October, 1936. He was British-bred, Am. Ch. Herzog of Evenlode, imported, trained and handled by Mrs. Richard Fort (later, Mrs. Jere Collins) owner of the Van Sandar Kennel in New York State.

Not long afterward, in May, 1937 to be exact, Mrs. Kenneth Fitzpatrick's owner-trained and shown American-bred Ch. Dirk Van Fitz finished his CD in California. Thus those two outstanding, early contributors to the breed in America as breeders and exhibitors in the conformation rings, also made Keeshond Obedience history within a few months of each other on opposite sides of the continent.

The next famous first for Kees in Obedience in this country was achieved in 1942. Virginia Liggett, who founded the well-known

Nether-Lair Kennel in Massachusetts and later became Mrs. Cowley, handled her Schoon to become the first Companion Dog Excellent (CDX). He was by Mrs. House's imported Ch. Guelder Gray Cloud ex Guelder Child of the Mist. And as related in *Chapter 5*, Schoon also completed his Utility Dog (UD) class work, but not the Tracking Tests necessary for a UD title at that time.

As the amount of breeding and public awareness of the breed as household companions slowly grew, interest in the Keeshond as an Obedience worker increased accordingly. But this took time. For many years, few Keeshonden were annually registered by the American Kennel Club.

The *total* Keeshond registrations for the 16 years from 1930 through 1945 were 612, an average of only 38 a year. During the next decade the annual average became 284 and in 1955 the breed ranked 43rd in relation to the number registered in other breeds that year. Though 2,010 Kees were recorded in 1968, other breeds had also increased and the Keeshond still ranked 43rd among the 116 AKC recognized breeds.

Milo and Margaret Pearsall are widely known in the Obedience trial world as two of the foremost authorities on the subject in the United States, and as popular trial judges. The book, *Dog Obedience Training* by Messrs. Pearsall and Leedham, published in 1958 has long been considered a classic. But many people may not know of Mr. and Mrs. Pearsall's prominent role as Keeshond owners.

The Pearsalls were introduced to the breed in 1949 when Mrs. Jean Vincent gave their son George a puppy bitch bred by A. J. Meshirer by Ch. Wynstraat's Schnapps ex Ch. Conwood Jacqueline. The puppy was given with the understanding that she would be trained and shown in Obedience and if good enough, would also be exhibited in the breed ring. She turned out to be definitely good enough on both counts and became Ch. Dutch Vixen of Paumanake CDX.

At the 1950 Keeshond of America Specialty held with the Long Island Kennel Club show under Mrs. Vera Fitzpatrick, "Dutchie" went WB for five points and then finished her CD that day with 1st in Novice and Highest Score in Trial.

The first Obedience Team formed in the United States, of four Keeshonden and their owner-handlers, represented The Keeshond Club of America and was started in 1951 with Milo Pearsall as

Keeshond Club of America Team, 1952. Miss Betty P. Dunn, Ch. Pat's Gay Blade, CDX; Mr. Milo Pearsall, captain, Ch. Dutch Vixen of Paumanake, CDX; Mr. E. J. Cummings III, Ch. Wynstraat's Cover Boy, UD; and Mrs. Margaret Pearsall, with Wynstraat's Ceiling Zero, CD.

trainer and Captain. Its members were E. J. Cummings III with Ch. Wynstraat's Cover Boy CDX (by Ch. Dirk Adams ex Ch. Wynstraat's Delft) ; Betty P. Dunn (later, Mrs. Cummings III) with Ch. Pat's Gay Blade CDX (Ch. Wynstraat's Schnapps ex Ch. Floret Adams) ; George Pearsall with Ch. Dutch Vixen of Paumanake CDX and Mrs. Margaret Pearsall with Wynstraat's Ceiling Zero CD (Nero van Beau ex Ch. Wynstraat's Delft) .

While Ed Cummings III was in the armed forces during the Korean War, Mrs. Cummings II added to breed history when she trained and handled her son's Ch. Cover Boy CDX, to make him, in 1953, the first UD Keeshond. And for a number of years Ch. Wynstraat's Cover Boy UD retained the distinction of being the *only champion* UD Keeshond. Mrs. Cummings also substituted for her

199

Mr. and Mrs. Roger Van Houten's Ch. Rovic's Chimney Blaze, UD.

son on the Team while he was away, and in 1963 she was appointed National Obedience Chairman of the Keeshond Club of America.

Mr. Pearsall took his son's place with Dutchie while George was at college. And in 1953 Mrs. Hazel Penny and her Woodland September Song CDX and Joan Gianinoto with her Dutch Holiday of Paumanake CD took part in some of the Team's exhibition work in the latter part of the year.

The Team continued through 1962 with various changes as to handlers and dogs. At one point the canine members were four breed champions with a total of 13 Obedience degrees among them—a title-holding record unequalled to date by any other breed's team known to the author.

The Keeshond Team was outstanding as the winner of numerous trials held by The Nassau (Long Island) Dog Training Club, The Dog Owners Training Club of Maryland, The Port Chester Obedience Training Club (Rye, N.Y.) and others. It also became famous for its wins in exhibition competitions held in the Yankee Stadium and Rockefeller Center in New York City and for its many performances given at hospitals, orphanages and other such establishments.

Mr. Pearsall with Dutch Vixen gave an obedience demonstration on Mrs. Hayes Blake Hoyt's series of TV programs on dogs when Mrs. Vincent's Ch. Wynstraat's Kerk was presented as a top-winning Keeshond of the time and this author was interviewed on the breed in general. Mr. Pearsall and Dutchie were also on the Dave Garroway *Today Show* in connection with the publication of the Pearsall Dog Obedience Training book.

With a citation for his contributions to the breed through his successful work as Captain and trainer of the national Club's Teams, The Keeshond Club of America voted that The Dog World Award for outstanding service be presented to Mr. Milo Pearsall.

The June, 1953 Obedience section of the American Kennel Club's *Pure-Bred Dogs, American Kennel Gazette* gave a noteworthy account of the performances at a Lake Shore Kennel Club all-breed show and trial in Indiana of four members of one Keeshond litter and their half-brother, all bred by Chester Cunningham.

Bonnie's Misty King CDX, trained and shown by Dorothy Cunningham scored 194½ in Open B. He also took Best of Breed in eight entries. In Novice B, Mrs. Victor Greenland's owner-trained and handled Dorche's Smokey Lo earned 196½. Kloo's Happy Scamp had 190 in Novice A, owner-trainer, Carolyn Mysliwy. Owner-bred Dorche's Silver, shown by Dorothy Cunningham scored 198 in Novice A. That was Ruff's Dusty Star's first show. She was owned, trained and shown by Raymond Ruff. Her score in Novice A was 195. No comment needed.

Starting in the 1950s, Mrs. Wilma Whitmore's activities in California literally put Obedience Kees in the spotlight on the West Coast. Her first Keeshonden were Van Bie Arlemina CD and Ch. Donner Van Bie CD obtained as youngsters from Mrs. Gladys Baldwin's Van Bie Kennel.

The committee for the selection of dogs to receive the annual Ken-L Ration *Dog Hero Awards* for valor named Ch. Donner as a recipient of the honor in 1958. But long before that, actually in 1954, Donner and Arlemina produced Mrs. Whitmore's Tuf Feo of Donmina, one of the early UD Kees in America.

"Tuffy", as he was called at home, not only became famous as a stage and TV personality, but was apparently well named. Example: at a trial in Fresno he took 1st in Utility. Then sat on a bee. The bee scored twice. But Tuffy carried on well enough to take third in Open. The next day at Bakersfield he was 2nd in Utility in spite of a puffy rear-end. How many dogs would even work after their "sitter" was stung?

Many Kees are clowns and "ham" actors at heart. Tuf Feo was evidently one of them. He took to his training for movie work and tricks as the proverbial duck takes to water. As a result, this handsome Keeshond was in great demand for his "acts" riding a toy horse, performing stunts with a monkey on his back, playing the role of Bat Masterson and all the rest of his extensive repertoire. And he and his owner contributed countless exhibitions for charitable organizations.

Mr. Louis Menninger of Huntington, Long Island first worked with dogs in the Coast Guard's K-9 training and detraining programs during World War II. In 1955 he purchased a six month old Keeshond puppy from Mrs. M. S. Davis named Park-Cliffe Cindy Van Pelt who was by Van Fitz Hals of Park-Cliffe ex Pat's Beware.

But Cindy had problems. She had been raised as just a kennel dog for the first six months of her life and needed to become accustomed to people and strange dogs. So her owner enrolled with her in an Obedience training class conducted by Mrs. E. J. Cummings II who was instrumental in starting Mr. Menninger and Cindy on the road to superlative success in the Obedience field.

Right from the beginning Cindy was a great performer. At her first Match show she tied for Highest Score in Trial with 199. That was in 1956. Seven years later, at her last trial she was 4th highest with 197. According to Mr. Menninger the years between were filled with ups and downs, but Cindy was an easy dog to train and work with because she always tried to please.

Cindy received The Dog World Award for earning CD in three straight trials with scores of 195 or better. She then completed CDX and UD and won her classes at least 26 times. On four occasions she won Highest Combined Score in Trial (scores in Open B and Utility combined). The high points of her work were rare achievements for any dog—three perfect scores of 200, attained near the end of her great career.

202

Ch. Dirck van Fitz, CD, wh. 1935. First Keeshond to earn C.D. on the West Coast. (Ch. Dynasty of Canford ex Tillie van Fitz of Canford). Breeder-owner: Vera Fitzpatrick.

As a youngster, Mrs. Cummings' home-bred Ch. Dirdon's Bruik-baar UD joined the Menninger family in 1956. Bruikbaar also received The Dog World Award for his CD in three shows, and with 199½ at one of them, he was Highest Scorer in Trial.

Mr. Menninger and Park-Cliffe Cindy Van Pelt UD were also members of the Keeshond Club of America's Team for several years and of the Suffolk Obedience Training Club's Exhibition Drill Team. His activities as an obedience trainer began in 1958 and led to his becoming an exceedingly popular American Kennel Club approved judge of all Obedience classes.

Mr. Menninger also served The Keeshond Club of America on its Board of Directors and as a Specialty Show Trophy Chairman, and in 1962 was the Club's first National Obedience Chairman.

Mr. and Mrs. Robert Blachnik's Van Gyzt Hans UD, sired by Ch. Van Fitz Bingo ex Van Gyzt Princess Anne was bred in California in 1956 by Mrs. Helen Geist, the Secretary of The Keeshond Club of Southern California for many years.

Hans earned The Dog World Award in connection with his CD title and three times had Highest Score in Trial. The approximately 100 Obedience trophies he won, included the Pasanita Obedience Club's cup for Highest Scoring dog in 1959.

In 1962 a Keeshond Team was formed in Massachusetts and for several years it represented The New England Dog Training Club with great success in inter-club team competitions throughout the eastern seaboard.

Miss Margaret Ambrose was Captain of the team and its canine membership was quite a family affair. Three of the dogs were half-brothers, all sired by the fourth member—Mrs. Ralph Porter's Ch. Nether-Lair's Tchortie CD. Tchortie was by Nether-Lair's Arnsdaag ex Nether-Lair's Inga de Gyselaer and had won Best of Breed in the 1959 Keeshond Club of America Specialty.

The other teammates were Miss Ambrose and Ch. Barr-Chri's Tchortson CDX who was out of Nether-Lair's Zelda; Pamela Elie and Ch. Barr-Chri's Tristan of Keeshof CDX, ex Ch. Aminda of Keeshof and Margaret Donoghue with Beauregard of Barr-Chri UD, ex Ruttkay Realization.

Among its most notable wins, The N.E.D.T. Club's Keeshond Team twice won the annual inter-club Sweepstakes over five other breed teams at the Suffolk Obedience Training Club Trial in Long Island. It also topped the Middlesex County Kennel Club Trial and gave many exhibition performances for dog clubs and charities.

In 1960 Mr. and Mrs. Walter Dayringer in northern California bred what turned out to be a remarkable litter in more ways than one. It was sired by Mrs. Blanche Matthews' Ch. Ruttkay Go Man Go out of the Dayringers' Ch. KC's Holland Dutchess, bought from Mrs. Chester Pierce.

The two males and the female the Dayringers kept were all record makers as dual title winners with high degrees. They became Ch. Jul-Day Von Diedrick UD, Ch. Jul-Day Ravensdown de Syl UD and the most sensational of all was Ch. Jul-Day Wunderlust de Sylvia UD who was called "Lustie" by her family.

Mrs. Dayringer started training Lustie when she was only three months old and at her first show when two days over six months, she won her first leg on CD with 197. Two weeks later she gained her second leg, scoring 196 and the following week completed CD with 198½ as 1st in Novice A, aged six months and 21 days. But that

Mr. and Mrs. Charles Mulock's Ch. Rikki van Armel, CD, the first champion C.D. Keeshond to take Best in Show in the United States (1961).

New England Dog Training Club Team, 1962. Ch. Barr-Chri's Tchortson van Dyke, CDX; Beauregard of Barr-Chri, UD; Ch. Barr-Chri's Tristan of Keeshof, CDX; and Ch. Nether-Lair's Tchortie, CD.

Mr. and Mrs. Robert Blachnik's Vany Gyzt Hans, UD.

was just the start of this bitch's whirlwind career which may well be a record for speedy achievement in Obedience.

At her debut in Open work on August 13th, 1961 she tied for 2nd Highest in Trial and won the run-off. In her next two trials she completed CDX with scores of 197 and 196½.

Lustie's first and second legs in Utility were won with 197 November 5th and 19th. Mrs. Dayringer related that "we goofed in the next three shows, so she did not complete her UD until February 25, 1962." Even so, Lustie earned three degrees within ten months. What is equally amazing is the fact that when all this started, her owners were newcomers to the Obedience rings.

Later in 1962, this exceptional Obedience performer also whizzed through to her championship in eight straight shows in four months. At the show where Lustie finished that title, she first scored 198 in Utility, then went into the breed ring and came out with a five-point major win as Winners Bitch, Best of Winners and Best of Opposite Sex. Thus, when Lustie was the ripe old age of one year and eight months, she had won her CD, CDX, UD and championship, all within 14 months.

After taking time out to raise a litter sired by Ch. Vangabang of Vorden which included two champions—one of them a Best in Show dog and winner of several Groups and placings—Ch. Jul-Day Wunderlust de Sylvia UD was the third highest ranking Obedience Keeshond in the country in 1966.

In 1959 Mr. and Mrs. Roger Van Houten in Elmhurst, Long Island, N.Y. bought their first pedigreed dog—a Keeshond. At that time they knew nothing of dog shows, Obedience, breeding or showing. But their desire and ability to learn quickly brought them unusual success in a very short time.

The fact that the Van Houtens' first five owner-bred, trained and handled Rovic Kennel Keeshond champions had a total of five CDs, two CDXs and a UD among them and four Group placings, made quite a name for those dogs, their breeders and the breed.

The Van Houtens' most brilliant star was Ch. Rovic's Chimney Blaze UD. Whelped in 1960, he was sired by Ch. Ruttkay's Chimney Sweep ex. Ch. Wynfomeer's Firedancer CDX. Blaze finished his championship in February, 1963. The next month he started and finished his CD in three consecutive trials and placed Group 4th the day he got the degree. He completed CDX in March, 1965 with

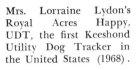

Mr. Thomas Ballen Jr.'s Van Bie Ponderosa Koningen, UD.

Mrs. Lorraine Lydon's Royal Acres Happy, UDT, the first Keeshond Utility Dog Tracker in the United States (1968).

a Highest Score in Trial and earned UD in June that year, winning Highest Combined Score. His record included nine Highest in Trial and eight Highest Combined Scores averaging 198½.

Mrs. Van Houten has held the position of National Obedience Recorder for the Keeshond Club of America since 1965, a time-consuming and exacting undertaking. To arrive at the annual ratings of every Keeshond in Obedience in the country, the American Kennel Club's records of each dog's scores in every Trial are used in conjunction with the *Blanche Saunders Point System* which is as follows: One point is given for qualifying scores (170 or more and in accordance with the AKC's Obedience regulations), plus 6 points for 1st place in the class, 5 for 2nd, 4 for 3rd and 3 for 4th. Highest Score in Trial brings 3 more points, Highest Combined Score (in Open B and Utility), 5 points, two 1sts (Open B and Utility) are worth 10 points.

In 1964 and 1965 Blaze was the top ranking Obedience Keeshond in the United States and the highest scoring Obedience *champion* Keeshond in 1966.

For the year 1964 Mr. and Mrs. Van Houten were awarded the Queensboro Kennel Club's trophies offered for the top winning, member-owned dogs in breed and in Obedience. And in 1965 an Obedience exhibition by Blaze with Mr. Van Houten handling as always, was a feature attraction at The Long Island Fair held at Roosevelt Raceway.

207

Mr. Louis Menninger's Park-Cliffe Cindy van Pelt, UD.

The news of the sudden death of this handsome pet and illustrious Obedience dog when less than six years old was received with sorrow by all who knew him.

Ch. Rovic's Chimney Blaze UD was bred only once. But in that litter whelped by Ch. Rovic's Lady Victoria, the three puppies shown indicated that through them, their sire had left a potentially important legacy. Ch. Rovic's Captain Blaze finished his breed title when he was just a year old. Rovic's Royal Blaze completed both CD and CDX in 1968. He placed in every trial and that same year

Mrs. Wilma Whitmore's Tuf Feo of Donmina, UD.

was runner-up to the top ranking Obedience Keeshond. At her first show, Rovic's Mighty Lady tied for Highest Score in Trial with brother Royal Blaze. She won the run-off and then her CD along with The Dog World Award.

The first dual titled Keeshond to win an all-breed Best in Show was Mr. and Mrs. Charles Mulock's Ch. Rikki Van Armel CD in Colorado. He was a son of Ch. Vangabang of Vorden out of Ch. Wilhelmina of Kittridge and bred by Mr. Walter Winkler. A few months later in 1961, the E. J. Cummings III's Ch. Wynstraat's Garry by Ch. Dirdon's Durk Donder out of Ch. Wynstraat's Delft, was retired from the breed ring at seven and a half years old after winning a Best in Show. Six weeks later, without ever having even heard the word "Heel" before, he was trained by his owners and completed CD. Who says you can't teach an old dog new tricks?

Mr. Thomas Ballen, Jr. of Englewood, Colorado with his Van Bie Ponderosa Koningen UD made an outstanding record for the breed in Obedience. Ponderosa was bred by Mrs. Gladys Baldwin in California and was by her Ch. Wilene First Knight ex Van Bie Missy Jo-Dee-O.

In 1964, about a year after Ponderosa was whelped, she was shown in four classes, won four 1sts, a perfect 200 and was twice Highest Scorer in Trial. The next year her scores in the seven classes entered averaged 197.7. In 1966 her success in 22 classes with another 200, a Highest Score and eight Highest Combined made her the highest ranking Keeshond in the country, a position she continued to hold in 1967 and 1968 until her retirement. 1968 was also the year that another Keeshond bitch earned a 200 score finishing her CD. It was Pandora of Redding owned by J. A. and R. D. Brown.

1964 was the year the first Keeshond acquired a Tracking Dog title. That history-making achievement was made by Miss Lorraine Skidmore of Litchfield, Connecticut, with her owner-bred-trained-and-handled Torlea's Dries Van Cover Boy CDX, who was both an American and Canadian CDX title holder.

Dries was a son of Ch. Wynfomeer's Cover Boy ex Dirdon's Lucretia van Hansel CD. Thus on his sire's side, Dries was a grandson of Ch. Wynstraat's Cover Boy, the first UD Keeshond.

It was not until 1968 that a Keeshond gained the full title of Utility Dog Tracker. The distinction of acquiring the highest of all Obedience degrees as the first and only UDT Keeshond went to Mrs.

Miss Lorraine Skidmore's Torlea's Dries van Cover Boy, CD, the first Keeshond Tracker in the United States.

Lorraine Lydon of Saratoga, California and her Royal Acres Happy, and was achieved at a San Francisco Dog Training Club trial in Oakland.

Happy, bred by Mrs. Frank G. Ketcham in 1959, was by Ch. Colonel Applejack of Carmel ex Keesdale Honey. His story, related by Mrs. Lydon, speaks for itself. She discovered Happy on a farm where he had apparently spent a large part of the first year of his life chained to a tractor in a field. Horrified by his physical condition and plight, she traded half a dozen bales of hay for him and his papers and took him home. After quite some time he was restored to normal condition by proper food and attention and became a full time, much loved house pet and successful Obedience dog.

Mr. and Mrs. Walter Dayringer's Ch. Jul-Day Ravensdown de Syl, UD, left, and Ch. Jul-Day Diederick, UD, right.

210

Mrs. Lydon also commented on the fact that he must have had inherently faultless temperament for it not to have been permanently harmed by the grim and important first year of his life when he evidently only had enough food and water to keep him alive and very little human companionship. And she went on to say, "He has always been a 'fun' dog to show, even when he goofs, and seems to enjoy the ring as much as I do."

On the occasion of the Nor-Cal Keeshond Club's first Specialty, Mrs. Lydon brought Happy out of retirement when he was nearly ten years old and gave him a bit of refresher training. The result— Royal Acres Happy UDT took Highest Score in Trial over 106 dogs with 198 in Open B at the all-breed Contra Costa County show—an added happy ending to the story.

Mrs. Gertrude Clemons, the Keeshond Club of America's Historian reported that in 1960 there were 10 CD degrees, 2 CDX and 1 UD completed by Kees. To give a general idea of the slow but steady increase in Keeshond activity in the Obedience rings in subsequent years, we cite Mrs. Van Houten's annual report covering 1968. In it we find that 72 different Kees made qualifying scores that year and it listed 37 new CD titles, 8 CDX, 2 UD and the 1 UDT earned.

The statistics compiled by Miss Eleanor Newhard from American Kennel Club records in regard to the number of champions sired and whelped by individual Keeshond studs and bitches during the 17 year period from June 1952 on, are interesting in an additional respect. They show that *approximately one out of every eight Keeshond champions also hold one or more Obedience titles.* This would appear to be a significant percentage of dual titlists for any breed, and contributes to the substantiation of the general belief that in the Keeshond, beauty and brains are combined to an unusual degree.

Keeshond Club of Southern California, first Specialty, 1952 at Los Angeles KC show. Posed before the benching is Mrs. Shirley Holdeman's baby in wagon drawn by Annetcha van Bie.

14

Keeshond Clubs
in the United States

THE Keeshond Club, which became the Keeshond Club of America, Inc., the parent club for the breed in the United States, was founded in 1935, in Chestnut Hill, a residential area of Philadelphia. Mrs. Irving Florsheim was named president, Mrs. L. W. Bonney and Mrs. Kenneth Fitzpatrick, vice-presidents, and Mrs. Henry Jarrett, secretary-treasurer. An official standard for the breed was submitted by the club and approved by the American Kennel Club in that same year of 1935, and served until it was slightly amended in 1949.

The first Keeshond Specialty was held in 1937 at the Ladies Kennel Association of America all-breed show in Long Island, N. Y. The Best of Breed over an entry of eight dogs, seven bitches, and two champions, judged by Oliver C. Harriman, was Mrs. Richard Fort's imported Am. Ch. Herzog of Evenlode. Winners Dog went to Mrs. Jarrett's Gerolf of Evenlode, and the Winners Bitch was Mrs. Fort's American-bred Anni Van Sandar. In those days there was no Best of Opposite Sex award, but a Keeshond Brace and Team were exhibited.

The first of two Keeshond Club of America Obedience Teams was formed in 1951 under the captaincy of Milo Pearsall. Both teams became successively famous as winners in competition with teams of other breeds, and through their exhibitions for charity in the East. A unique feature of one of the Keeshond teams was that each of its four members were both bench and Obedience title-holders.

Starting in 1962, the parent club inaugurated many programs to serve its members, the breed as a whole, and the local clubs which had been formed in various sections of the country. Standing committees were appointed to supervise: a Breeders' Code of Ethics, a Puppy Futurity Stake, National Publicity, National Obedience, National Trophies, By-Law Revision and Membership Admission. Pamphlets and leaflets were produced for general distribution and made available to owners and clubs at, or under, cost on such subjects as: the breed's history and characteristics; pictorial illustration of Rights and Wrongs to look for in interpreting the Standard; grooming; leash training; and newspaper publicity. Club Bulletins were issued three times a year, and in 1965 the first *Keeshond Review* was published. The award of KCA Medals of Achievement for bench and Obedience titles completed by the dogs of members was established, and the club's seal and membership pin were produced.

Through the members' generous response to the national trophy program, trophies have been offered annually for top-winning member-owned bench and Obedience Kees, and for "stud of the year" and other breeding achievements. Two Challenge Trophies were also given to the club: Mr. and Mrs. E. J. Cummings III's Wynfomeer Trophy for Best in Futurity; and from Mrs. Doreen Anderson, a Scottish breeder and judge, the Kultz Challenge Cup for the member-breeder of the most champions finished during a year.

The first Puppy Futurity Stake was held in 1965 at Ladies Kennel Association with 20 entries judged by Mrs. Gladys Baldwin. Best in Futurity was Rodney Nickerson's Keenic's Turf Commander and Mrs. Charles Stoodley's bitch, Coventry's Wintempest went BOS.

The Futurities were a popular addition to the national Club's Specialties. They brought much prestige and cash to successful participants and have been credited with being the fourth richest Puppy Stakes of any breed in the country.

It was evident in 1962 that in many parts of the country Keeshonden were being raised and sold on a wholesale basis by so-called "breeders", who were either utterly callous to, or unaware of, the potentially harmful effects of their operations on their own reputations, as well as on the welfare of the puppies involved, and on the breed. The club therefore passed a resolution "strongly disapproving" such practices, and established an Ethics Committee. The efforts of the Committee and members of the Board of Directors resulted in a Code of Ethics as a Breeders' Guide, compiled for the benefit of breeders, owners, and potential owners of Keeshonden. The Code was adopted by the Keeshond Club of America's membership in 1966 and was incorporated in the revised By-Laws and new membership application and sponsor's form put into effect in 1967.

The Pacific Coast Keeshond Club was formed by ten enthusiasts in 1940. It was the second club in the country and the first to be an affiliate of the Keeshond Club of America. Mrs. Kenneth Fitzpatrick, who introduced the breed on the West Coast in 1932, was elected president, Mrs. Mancel Clark was made vice-president, and George J. Davis became secretary-treasurer. The first Specialty was held with the 1940 Harbor Cities show where the 21 entries, happily benched together on one long, undivided bench, caused a sensation. The top winners under judge Chris Shuttleworth were Mrs. Fitzpatrick's Ch. Dirk Van Fitz CD, who placed third in the Group, and the Mancel Clark's puppy, Sanka, who was BOS.

Due to World War II there was little club activity for some time, though occasional meetings were held and breeding continued. In 1950 the club was reorganized as The Keeshond Club of Southern California, with Mr. Davis as president, A. J. Kaufmann, vice-president, Mrs. Gladys Baldwin as secretary-treasurer, and Mrs. Fitzpatrick, Mrs. Van Cott Niven (later, Mrs. Porter Washington), and Lawrence P. Smith as Directors. Since the reorganization, annual Specialties have been held with steadily increasing entries, and the club has won many prizes for its decorated benches. The club's program at meetings, training classes, Matches, Specialties, Obedience Team, Kees Komments Newsletter, publicity program and other activities, combined with the great bench and Obedience record of members' Kees, have made The Keeshond Club of Southern California an important factor in the breed's progress on the West Coast.

The Capital Keeshond Club was the next to be affiliated with the parent club. It was organized in Maryland in 1957 with 10 charter members under the presidency of James MacMartin, with Mrs.

Ronald West and Mrs. David Carey as vice-presidents, and Mrs. Lois McNamara as secretary-treasurer.

Its first Specialty was a record-setting show-stopper in 1961 with 65 Kees benched without dividers in front of a sky-blue backdrop at the National Capital Kennel Club all-breed show in Washington, D.C. Judge Derek Rayne chose Mrs. Gertrude Clemons' Ch. Theo v. Hergert as BOB, Mrs. West's Ch. Andante of Westcrest as BOS, the E. P. Hempsteads' Nederlan Herman v. Mack as BOW, and Marilyn Bender's Wil-Los Zoet Zang as WB. The club's Specialty was the first in the country to draw an entry of over 60 Kees, and Capital was the first local Kees Club to have a British judge officiate at its Specialty, Mrs. Doreen Anderson having had that honor.

Highlights of the Capital Keeshond Club's other activities have been its Newsletter, a publicity leaflet entitled *What Is a Keeshond?*, and the club's seal and membership pin. Two Challenge Trophies have been donated as expressions of esteem for the club: The Alfred McCormack Memorial Trophy, given by Mrs. McCormack for BOB at the Capital Keeshond Club Specialties; and the Kultz Trophy, given by Mrs. Anderson for the member-owner of the Keeshond which wins BOB over the highest total of entries during the calendar year and has competed in the CKC's Specialty that year.

The Keesond Club of Delaware Valley has made breed history in many ways. Under the leadership of John A. Lafore, Jr. as president, 15 fanciers in the Pennsylvania area launched the club in 1960. Mrs. Virginia Ruttkay, R. Thomas Knapp, and Mrs. Max Goebel were named vice-presidents; Mrs. Maren McClendon, secretary; and Mrs. J. Hale, treasurer.

Only two years later the club was approved by the American Kennel Club to hold a Specialty at Devon, Pa. and was elected an affiliate of the parent club. The 99 regular entries in the KCDV's first show exceeded all previous records in American shows, and were judged by the author. The Wm. McNamara's Ch. Wil-Los Jamie Boy took BOB; Marilyn Bender's Ch. Wil-Los Zoet Zang, BOS; John Schuessler's Ruttkay Tannenbaum von Sturm, BOW, and Miss Bender's Mar-I-Ben Kotton Kandy, WB. From then on, the Club broke its own entry records each year. The 1969 entry had 183 dogs in the regular competition under Mrs. Patricia M. Marcmann.

The KCDV's newsletter, *Kee Topics,* originally came out in mimeographed form in 1962. It was edited and distributed to other

216

Officers and directors of the Keeshond Club of Southern California for the years 1956–1957, posed with their dogs.

Keeshond clubs' members by Mr. and Mrs. William D. Westcott, and soon became an excellent, handsomely printed and well illustrated magazine with wide coverage of news of Kees and breed clubs. *Kee Topics* was the first such publication devoted exclusively to the breed and the magazine's popularity led to an extensive circulation.

The Nor-Cal Keeshond Club, Inc. was started in 1961 in Pleasanton, California by 51 charter members who elected Gerald Barrett the first year's president; Gaston Loftin, vice-president; Mrs. Blanche Matthews, secretary; and Mrs. Gilbert Andrews, treasurer. Since then the club has done a great deal for the breed in northern California.

Awards to members whose Kees complete championship and/or Obedience titles began in 1963, and the club-supported Keeshond entries in area shows resulted in a phenomenal increase in the number exhibited. An example was the 1964 Golden Gate show in San Francisco with 36, a jump of more than 25 over the entries of previous years. The Nor-Cal benches were also decorated at most shows, which brought additional public attention to the breed and won many prizes.

The club's matches drew record-making entries of from 45 to 113. An unusual feature of an early "Fun Match" was a pamphlet containing practical information, wittily written and illustrated with cartoons by members. Chapters were titled: "Should We Breed Our Girl?"; "Must Our Boy Be A Stud?"; "And Now We Have Puppies!"; "What Are 'Papers'?" The pamphlet, plus a verbal explanation of ring procedure given at ringside, a Junior Handling competition,

A Parade of Champions at a sanction match of the Keeshond Club of Southern California held at the R.K.O. movie studios in 1951. Actress Marie Wilson (fourth from left) and actor Jack Buetel (second from right) pose with the owners and their champions.

and a demonstration on training a conformation Brace, made that 1964 Match an outstanding affair.

Nor-Cal's first Specialty was a great success at Contra Costa in 1969 with 82 entries for 71 Kees under judge Charles Mulock. The top winners were Ralph Sims' Ch. Zeedrift Kwikzilver, who also won the Group, and the Walter Dayringers' Ch. Jul-Day Treurig Sara CD, BOS. Stanley Roberts' Van Bie Top Hat And Spats took BOW and the George Melchiors Velvet Touch of Algernon was the WB.

The first meeting of the Keeshond Club of Big D, as it was first called, was held in Dallas, Texas in 1959, with nine people present. John Hevron was made president, and Mrs. Marjorie Sampson, corresponding secretary. Meetings were held fairly regularly and entries in the Dallas and Fort Worth shows were encouraged. In 1965, the club took an upsurge as owners in many parts of the state became interested in the endeavors to promote the breed.

The club's name was changed to The Keeshond Club of Dallas in 1966, and the first B Match was held in December of that year. This was followed by two more B's in 1967, and two A's in 1968. Then came the American Kennel Club's approval to hold a licensed Specialty in Dallas in 1969, and the Dallas Club became the fifth local club to be made an affiliate of the Keeshond Club of America.

The Dallas Specialty has the distinction of being the first Keeshond Specialty in America to be held separately from an all-breed kennel club show, and was completely staged and managed by the breed club's members. Among the top stars in the 38 entries under Miss Dorothy D. Nickles was Mr. and Mrs. Peter Davis's Merrikee Wrocky Royal Rogue. He was handled to WD, BOW and BOB by nine-year-old Kathleen Winslow, and Mrs. Gwen Worley's owner-bred and handled Quaint Fancy took WB and BOS.

We are indebted to Mrs. Elmer H. White, 1969 vice-president and show secretary, for the foregoing information. Mrs. White also wrote that "the asset most difficult to put in words is the wonderful spirit which prevails throughout the membership. Although scattered over Texas, with a few members in Louisiana and Oklahoma, and distances of 300 and 400 miles separating members from Dallas, the whole group works together with great enthusiasm and gets behind the club's objectives. The bulk of the work has naturally had to be done locally, and we are fortunate in having members in Dallas who enjoy their work for the club and the breed. But much of the progress made has been due to widespread interest and support."

A number of other Keeshond clubs made great strides in the 1960s toward holding Specialties. These clubs, with names of their first presidents, are:

Evergreen, *in the Washington-Oregon area,* Roy Horton.
Heritage Trail, *Massachusetts,* Mrs. Harriet Ovington.
Heart of America, *Missouri,* Dr. Marc Lampi.
Buckeye, *Ohio,* Frank E. Vinion.

In addition, up-and-coming groups of breed enthusiasts have formed clubs in Houston, Texas; northern Illinois; and in Michigan.

Every Keeshond club in the country is to be congratulated on the fact that they and their members' personal efforts in behalf of the breed have been vital factors in the Keeshond's progress in America.

Whether you are a novice, a long-time pet owner, an exhibitor, a breeder, or an obedience "buff", much pleasure and knowledge is to be gained from club membership. It brings you the advantage of association with other Keeshond owners and the programs and services available from The Keeshond Club of America or a local club, or both. The American Kennel Club, 51 Madison Avenue, New York, N. Y. 10010, will send you the name and address of the current secretary of The Keeshond Club of America, to whom you can write for information on applying for membership in either the national or a local club.

15

The Specialty Winners
in Picture

1953. Mr. J. Whitney Peterson and Ch. Nederland Keesa v. Banner, BOS. Miss Kathleen Staples, judge. Mrs. Jean Vincent and Ch. Wynstraat's Kerk, BOB.

1954. Roy Holloway with Mrs. J. Whitney Peterson's Ch. Nether Lair's Banner de Gyselaer, BOB. Mrs. Hayes Hoyt, judge. Mr. John Drake and Holland-Honds Tina v. Banner, BOS.

1955. Mrs. Warner Hays, judge. Mrs. J. Whitney Peterson and Bacchus of Evenlode, BOB.

1956. Mrs. Richard Koehne and Ch. Van Ons Early Burly, BOS. Mrs. Russell Thompson, judge. Mrs. E. J. Cummings II and Ch. Dirdon's Durk Donder, BOB.

1957. Mrs. E. J. Cummings II and Ch. Dirdon's Durk Donder, BOB. Mrs. L. W. Bonney, judge. Mrs Betty Dunn Cummings with Mrs R. Koehne's Ch. Van Ons Balda, BOS.

1958. Roy Holloway with Mrs. Alfred McCormack's Ch. Keeshaven's Clown, BOB. Mr. Russell Thompson, judge. Mrs. E. J. Cummings II and Ch. Dirdon's Kostbaar, BOS.

1959. Miss M. Ambrose with Mrs. Ralph Porter's Ch. Nether-Lair's Tchortie CD, BOB. Miss Kathleen Staples, judge. Mrs. J. Whitney Peterson and Nederlan Peppa, BOW and BOS.

1960. Mrs. E. J. Cummings II and Ch. Hanzel v. Dohrmann CD, BOB. Mr. Leo Wilson, judge. Mrs. Jane West and Ruttkay Winsome, **BOS.**

1961. Left, Roy Holloway with Mrs. Gertrude Clemons' Ch. Theo v. Hargert, BOB. Mrs. Milton Erlanger, judge. Right, Mrs. Christopher Becker and Nederlan Linda van Keeshof, BOW and BOS.

1962. Left, Mr. Maxwell Riddle, judge. Mrs. R. B. Hollaman and Ch. Kenmerk Hallmark, BOB. Right, Mrs. J. Whitney Peterson and Ch. Volaura of Vorden, BOS.

1963. Mrs. J. Whitney Peterson and Ch. Volaura of Vorden, BOS. Mrs. E. J. Cummings II, judge. Mrs. Nancy Riley with Mrs. Carl Gettig's Ch. Vereeren of Vorden, BOB.

1964. W. D. Westcott with Mr. and Mrs. Carl Gettig's Ch. Vereeren of Vorden, BOB. Mrs. J. Whitney Peterson, judge. Mr. Philip Shoudy and Ch. Mar-I-Ben Butterscotch, BOS.

1965. Mrs. Nancy Riley and Ch. Von Storm's Emaria, BOS Mr. Kenneth Given, judge. Roy Holloway with Mr. and Mrs. E. P. Hempstead's Ch. Nederlan Herman v. Mack, BOB.

1966. Left, Mrs. Paul Silvernail, judge. Roy Holloway with Mr. and Mrs. E. P. Hempstead's Ch. Von Storm's Emerson Prince Piet, BOB. Right, Mrs. Nancy Riley's Ch. Wallbridge's Best Bet, BOS.

1967. Left, Mrs. Florence Broadhurst, judge. Roy Holloway with Mr. and Mrs. E. P. Hempstead's Ch. Von Storm's Emerson Prince Piet, BOB. Right, Mrs. Dolores Scharff and Ch. Ruttkay Zilver Frost Van Roem, BOS.

1968. Left, Mr. Charles Mulock, judge, Mrs. Carl Gettig and Ch. Vereeren of Vorden, BOB. Right, Mrs. E. K. Olafson and Rugosa of Rhinevale, BOS.

1969. Mr. and Mrs. Stuart Duncan's Ch. Waakzaam Wollenhoven, BOB. The judge was Miss Melba Jones, and Mrs. Olafson's Can. Ch. Rugosa of Rhinevale was BOW and again BOS.

Chris Blom

The following pages are excerpted from the book "General Care and Training of Your Dog" by Elsworth S. Howell, Milo G. Denlinger and A. C. Merrick, D.V.M., and are included as a supplemental guide to good care of your Keeshond.

16

Training and Simple Obedience

E VERY DOG that is mentally and physically sound can be taught good manners and simple obedience by any normal man, woman, or child over eight years old.

Certain requirements must be met by the dog, trainer and the environment if the training is to be enjoyable and effective. The dog must be rested and calm. The trainer must be rested, calm, gentle, firm, patient and persistent. The training site should be dry, comfortable and, except for certain exercises, devoid of distractions.

Proper techniques can achieve quick and sure results. Always use short, strong words for commands and always use the *same* word or words for the same command. Speak with authority; never scream or yell. Teach one command or exercise at a time and make sure the dog understands it and performs it perfectly before you proceed to the next step. Demand the dog's undivided attention; if he wavers or wanders, speak his name or pat him smartly or jerk his leash. Use pats and praise plentifully; avoid tidbit training if at all possible because tidbits may not always be available in an emergency and the dog will learn better without them. Keep lessons short; when the dog begins to show boredom, stop and do not resume in less than two hours. One or two ten-minute lessons a day should be ample, especially for a young puppy. Dogs have their good and bad days; if your well dog seems unduly lazy, tired, bored or off-color, put off the lesson until tomorrow. Try to make lessons a joy, a happy time both for you and the dog, but do demand and get the desired action. Whenever correction or punishment is needed, use ways and devices that the dog does not connect with you; some of these means are given in the following instructions. Use painful punishment only as a last resort.

"NO!"

The most useful and easily understood command is "NO!" spoken in a sharp, disapproving tone and accompanied with a shaking finger. At first, speak the dog's name following with "NO!" until the meaning of the word—your displeasure—is clear.

"COME!"

Indoors or out, let the dog go ten or more feet away from you. Speak his name following at once with "COME!" Crouch, clap your hands, pick up a stick, throw a ball up and catch it, or create any other diversion which will lure the dog to you. When he comes, praise and pat effusively. As with all commands and exercises repeat the lesson, until the dog *always* comes to you.

THE FIRST NIGHTS

Puppies left alone will bark, moan and whine. If your dog is not to have the run of the house, put him in a room where he can do the least damage. Give him a Nylabone and a strip of beef hide (both available in supermarkets or pet shops and excellent as teething pacifiers). A very young puppy may appreciate a loud-ticking clock which, some dog trainers say, simulates the heart-beat of his former litter mates. Beyond providing these diversions, grit your teeth and steel your heart. If in pity you go to the howling puppy, he will howl every time you leave him. Suffer one night, two nights or possibly three, and you'll have it made.

The greatest boon to dog training and management is the wooden or wire crate. Any two-handed man can make a ⅜″ plywood crate. It needs only four sides, a top, a bottom, a door on hinges and with a strong hasp, and a fitting burlap bag stuffed with shredded newspaper, cedar shavings or 2″ foam rubber. Feed dealers or seed stores should give you burlap bags; be sure to wash them thoroughly to remove any chemical or allergy-causing material. The crate should be as long, as high and three times as wide as the dog will be full grown. The crate will become as much a sanctuary to your dog as a cave was to his prehistoric ancestor; it will also help immeasurably in housebreaking.

HOUSEBREAKING

The secret to housebreaking a healthy normal dog is simple: take him out every hour if he is from two to six months old when you get him; or the first thing in the morning, immediately after every meal, and the last thing at night if he is over six months.

For very young puppies, the paper break is indicated. Lay eight or ten layers of newspapers in a room corner most remote from the puppy's bed. By four months of age or after two weeks in a new home if older, a healthy puppy should not need the paper *IF* it is exercised outdoors often and *IF* no liquid (including milk) is given after 5 P.M. and *IF* it is taken out not earlier than 10 P.M. at night and not later than 7 A.M. the next morning.

When the dog does what it should when and where it should, praise, praise and praise some more. Be patient outdoors: keep the dog out until action occurs. Take the dog to the same general area always; its own traces and those of other dogs thus drawn to the spot will help to inspire the desired action.

In extreme cases where frequent exercising outdoors fails, try to catch the dog in the act and throw a chain or a closed tin can with pebbles in it near the dog but not on him; say "NO!" loudly as the chain or can lands. In the most extreme case, a full 30-second spanking with a light strap may be indicated but be sure you catch the miscreant *in the act*. Dog memories are short.

Remember the crate discussed under "THE FIRST NIGHTS." If you give the dog a fair chance, he will NOT soil his crate.

Do not rub his nose in "it." Dogs have dignity and pride. It is permissible to lead him to his error as soon as he commits it and to remonstrate forcefully with "NO!"

17

The Breeding of Dogs

HERE, if anywhere in the entire process of the care and management of dogs, the exercise of good judgment is involved. Upon the choice of the two dogs, male and female, to be mated together depends the future success or failure of one's dogs. If the two to be mated are ill chosen, either individually or as pertains to their fitness as mates, one to the other, all the painstaking care to feed and rear the resultant puppies correctly is wasted. The mating together of two dogs is the drafting of the blueprints and the writing of the specifications of what the puppies are to be like. The plans, it is true, require to be executed; the puppies, when they arrive, must be adequately fed and cared for in order to develop them into the kinds of dogs they are in their germ plasm designed to become. However, if the plans as determined in the mating are defective, just so will the puppies that result from them be defective, in spite of all the good raising one can give them.

The element of luck in the breeding of dogs cannot be discounted, for it exists. The mating which on paper appears to be the best possible may result in puppies that are poor and untypical of their breed. Even less frequently, a good puppy may result from a chance mating together of two ill chosen parents. These results are fortuitous and unusual, however. The best dogs as a lot come from parents carefully chosen as to their individual excellences and as to their suitability as mates for each other. It is as unwise as

233

it is unnecessary to trust to luck in the breeding of dogs. Careful planning pays off in the long run, and few truly excellent dogs are produced without it.

Some breeders without any knowledge of genetics have been successful, without knowing exactly why they succeeded. Some of them have adhered to beliefs in old wives' tales and to traditional concepts that science has long since exploded and abandoned. Such as have succeeded have done so in spite of their lack of knowledge and not because of it.

There is insufficient space at our disposal in this book to discuss in detail the science of genetics and the application of that science to the breeding of dogs. Whole books have been written about the subject. One of the best, clearest, and easiest for the layman to understand is *The New Art of Breeding Better Dogs,* by Philip Onstott, which may be obtained from Howell Book House, the publisher. In it and in other books upon the subject of genetics will be found more data about the practical application of science to the breeding of livestock than can be included here.

The most that can be done here is to offer some advice soundly based upon the genetic laws. Every feature a dog may or can possess is determined by the genes carried in the two reproductive cells, one from each parent, from the union of which he was developed. There are thousands of pairs of these determiners in the life plan of every puppy, and often a complex of many genes is required to produce a single recognizable attribute of the dog.

These genes function in pairs, one member of each pair being contributed by the father and the other member of the pair coming from the mother. The parents obtained these genes they hand on from their parents, and it is merely fortuitous which half of any pair of genes present in a dog's or a bitch's germ plasm may be passed on to any one of the progeny. Of any pair of its own genes, a dog or a bitch may contribute one member to one puppy and the other member to another puppy in the same litter or in different litters. The unknown number of pairs of genes is so great that there is an infinite number of combinations of them, which accounts for the differences we find between two full brothers or two full sisters. In fact, it depends upon the genes received whether a dog be a male or a female.

We know that the male dog contributes one and the bitch the

other of every pair of genes that unite to determine what the puppy will be like and what he will grow into. Thus, the parents make exactly equal contributions to the germ plasm or zygote from which every puppy is developed. It was long believed that the male dog was so much more important than the bitch in any mating that the excellence or shortcomings of the bitch might be disregarded. This theory was subsequently reversed and breeders considered the bitch to be more important than the dog. We now know that their contribution in every mating and in every individual puppy is exactly equal, and neither is to be considered more than the other.

There are two kinds of genes—the recessive genes and the dominant. And there are three kinds of pairs of genes: a recessive from the sire plus a recessive from the dam; a dominant from the sire plus a dominant from the dam; and a dominant from one parent plus a recessive from the other. It is the last combination that is the source of our trouble in breeding. When both members of a pair of genes are recessive, the result is a recessive attribute in the animal that carries them; when both members of the pair are dominant, the result is a pure dominant attribute; but when one member of the pair is recessive and the other member dominant, the result will be a wholly or only partially dominant attribute, which will breed true only half of the time. This explains why a dog or a bitch may fail to produce progeny that looks at all like itself.

If all the pairs of a dog's genes were purely dominant, we could expect him to produce puppies that resembled himself in all particulars, no matter what kind of mate he was bred to. Or if all his genes were recessive and he were mated to a bitch with all recessive genes, the puppies might be expected to look quite like the parents. However, a dog with mixed pairs of genes bred to a bitch with mixed pairs of genes may produce anything at all, puppies that bear no resemblance to either parent.

Long before the Mendelian laws were discovered, some dogs were known to be "prepotent" to produce certain characters, that is the characters would show up in their puppies irrespective of what their mates might be like. For instance, some dogs, themselves with dark eyes, might be depended upon never to produce a puppy with light eyes, no matter how light eyed the mate to which he was bred. This was true despite the fact that the dog's litter brother which had equally dark eyes, when bred to a light eyed bitch might produce a large percentage of puppies with light eyes.

Before it is decided to breed a bitch, it is well to consider whether she is worth breeding, whether she is good enough as an individual and whether she came from a good enough family to warrant the expectations that she will produce puppies worth the expense and trouble of raising. It is to be remembered that the bitch contributes exactly half the genes to each of her puppies; if she has not good genes to contribute, the time and money involved in breeding her and rearing her puppies will be wasted.

It is conceded that a bad or mediocre bitch when bred to an excellent dog will probably produce puppies better than herself. But while one is "grading up" from mediocre stock, other breeders are also grading upward from better stock and they will keep just so far ahead of one's efforts that one can never catch up with them. A merely pretty good bitch is no good at all for breeding. It is better to dispose of a mediocre bitch or to relegate her to the position of a family pet than to breed from her. It is difficult enough, with all the care and judgment one is able to muster, to obtain superlative puppies even from a fine bitch, without cluttering the earth with inferior puppies from just any old bitch.

If one will go into the market and buy the best possible bitch from the best possible family one's purse can afford and breed her sensibly to the best and most suitable stud dog one can find, success is reasonably sure. Even if for economy's sake, the bitch is but a promising puppy backed up by the best possible pedigree, it will require only a few months until she is old enough to be bred. From such a bitch, one may expect first-rate puppies at the first try, whereas in starting with an inferior bitch one is merely lucky if in two or three generations he obtains a semblance of the kind of dog he is trying to produce.

Assuming it is decided that the bitch is adequate to serve as a brood bitch, it becomes necessary to choose for her a mate in collaboration with which she may realize the ultimate of her possibilities. It is never wise to utilize for stud the family pet or the neighbor's pet just because he happens to be registered in the studbook or because his service costs nothing. Any dog short of the best and most suitable (wherever he may be and whoever may own him) is an extravagance. If the bitch is worth breeding at all, she is worth shipping clear across the continent, if need be, to obtain for her a mate to enable her to realize her possibilities. Stud fees may range from fifty to one hundred dollars or even more. The average value of each puppy, if well reared, should at the time of weaning approximate the legitimate stud fee of its sire. With a good bitch it is therefore profitable to lay out as much as may be required to obtain the services of the best and most suitable stud dog—always assuming that he is worth the price asked. However, it is never wise to choose an inferior or unsuitable dog just because he is well ballyhooed and commands an exorbitant stud fee.

There are three considerations by which to evaluate the merits of a stud dog—his outstanding excellence as an individual, his pedigree and the family from which he derived, and the excellence or inferiority of the progeny he is known to have produced.

As an individual a good stud dog may be expected to be bold and aggressive (not vicious) and structurally typical of his breed, but without any freakish exaggerations of type. He must be sound, a free and true mover, possess fineness and quality, and be a gentleman of his own breed. Accidentally acquired scars or injuries such as broken legs should not be held against him, because he can transmit only his genes to his puppies and no such accidents impair his genes.

A dog's pedigree may mean much or little. One of two litter brothers, with pedigrees exactly alike, may prove to be a superlative show and stud dog, and the other worth exactly nothing for either purpose. The pedigree especially is not to be judged on its length, since three generations is at most all that is required, although further extension of the pedigree may prove interesting to a curious owner. No matter how well-bred his pedigree may show a dog to be, if he is not a good dog the ink required to write the pedigree was wasted.

The chief value of a pedigree is to enable us to know from which of a dog's parents, grandparents, or great-grandparents, he derived his merits, and from which his faults. In choosing a mate for him (or for her, as the case may be) one seeks to reinforce the one and to avoid the other. Let us assume that one of the grandmothers was upright in shoulder, whereas the shoulder should be well laid back; we can avoid as a mate for such a dog one with any

237

tendency to straight shoulders or one from straight shouldered ancestry. The same principle would apply to an uneven mouth, a light eye, a soft back, splayed feet, cowhocks, or to any other inherited fault. Suppose, on the other hand, that the dog himself, the parents, and all the grandparents are particularly nice in regard to their fronts; in a mate for such a dog, one desires as good a front as is obtainable, but if she, or some of her ancestors are not too good in respect to their fronts, one may take a chance anyway and trust to the good fronted dog with his good fronted ancestry to correct the fault. That then is the purpose of the pedigree as a guide to breeding.

A stud dog can best be judged, however, by the excellence of the progeny he is known to have produced, if it is possible to obtain all the data to enable the breeder to evaluate that record. A complete comparative evaluation is perhaps impossible to make, but one close enough to justify conclusions is available. Not only the number but the quality of the bitches to which the dog has been bred must enter into the consideration. A young dog may not have had the opportunity to prove his prowess in the stud. He may have been bred to few bitches and those few of indifferent merits, or his get may not be old enough as yet to hit the shows and establish a record for themselves or for their sire. Allowance may be made for such a dog.

On the other hand, a dog may have proved himself to be phenomenal in the show ring, or may have been made to seem phenomenal by means of the owner's ballyhoo and exploitation. Half of the top bitches in the entire country may have been bred to him upon the strength of his winning record. Merely from the laws of probability such a dog, if he is not too bad, will produce some creditable progeny. It is necessary to take into consideration the opportunities a dog has had in relation to the fine progeny he has produced.

That, however, is the chief criterion by which a good stud dog may be recognized. A dog which can sire two or three excellent puppies in every litter from a reasonably good bitch may be considered as an acceptable stud. If he has in his lifetime sired one or two champions each year, and especially if one or two of the lot are superlative champions, top members of their breed, he is a great stud dog. Ordinarily and without other considerations, such a dog is to be preferred to one of his unproved sons, even though the son be as good or better an individual. In this way one employs genes one knows to produce what one wants. The son may be only hybrid dominant for his excellent qualities.

In the choice of a stud dog no attention whatever need be paid to claims that he sires numerically big litters. Unless the sire is deficient in sperm, the number of puppies in the litter, provided there are any puppies at all, depends entirely upon the bitch. At one service, a dog deposits enough spermatozoa to produce a million puppies, if there were so many ova to be fertilized. In any event, the major purpose should be to obtain good puppies, not large numbers of them.

There are three methods of breeding employed by experienced breeders—outcrossing, inbreeding, and line breeding. By outcrossing is meant the breeding together of mates of which no blood relationship can be traced. It is much favored by novice breeders, who feel that the breeding together of blood relatives is likely to result in imbecility, constitutional weakness, or some other kind of degeneration. Inbreeding is the mating together of closely related animals—father to daughter, mother to son, brother to sister, half brother to half sister. Some of the best animals ever produced have been bred from some such incestuous mating, and the danger from such practices, if they are carried out by persons who know what they are about, is minimal. Line breeding is the mating together of animals related one to another, but less closely—such as first cousins, grandsire to granddaughter, granddam to grandson, uncle to niece, or aunt to nephew.

Absolute outcrossing is usually impossible, since all the good dogs in any breed are more or less related—descended from some common ancestor in the fifth or sixth or seventh generation of their pedigrees. In any event, it is seldom to be recommended, since the results from it in the first generation of progeny are usually not satisfactory. It may be undertaken by some far-sighted and experienced breeder for the purpose of bringing into his strain some particular merit lacking in it and present in the strain of the unrelated dog. While dogs so bred may obtain an added vigor from what is known in genetics as *heterosis*, they are likely to manifest a coarseness and a lack of uniformity in the litter which is not to be found in more closely bred puppies. Good breeders never outcross if it is possible to obtain the virtues they want by sticking to their own strain. And when they do outcross, it is for the purpose of utilizing the outcrossed product for further breeding. It is not an end in itself.

Inbreeding (or incest breeding, as it is sometimes called) involves no such hazards as are and in the past have been attributed to it. It produces some very excellent dogs when correctly employed, some very bad ones even when correctly employed, and all bad ones when carelessly used. All the standard breeds of dogs were established as uniform breeds through intense inbreeding and culling over many generations. Inbreeding brings into manifestation undesirable recessive genes, the bearers of which can be discarded and the strain can thus be purged of its bad recessives.

Dogs of great soundness and excellence, from excellent parents and grandparents, all of them much alike, may be safely mated together, no matter how closely they may be related, with reasonable hope that most of the progeny will be sound and typical with a close resemblance to all the members of their ancestry. However, two such superlative and well-bred dogs are seldom to be found. It is the way to make progress rapidly and to establish a strain of dogs much alike and which breeds true. The amateur with the boldness and courage to try such a mating in the belief that his dogs are good enough for it is not to be discouraged. But if his judgment is not justified by the results, let him not complain that he has not been warned.

Line breeding is the safest course between the Scylla of outcrossing and the Charybdis of inbreeding for the inexperienced navigator in the sea of breeding. It, too, is to be used with care, because when it succeeds it partakes much of the nature of inbreeding. At any rate, its purpose is the pairing of like genes.

Here the pedigrees come into use. We examine the pedigree of the bitch to be bred. We hope that all the dogs named in it are magnificent dogs, but we look them over and choose the best of the four grandparents. We check this grandparent's breeding and find it good, as it probably is if it is itself a dog or bitch of great excellence. We shall assume that this best dog in the bitch's pedigree is the maternal grandsire. Then our bitch may be bred back to this particular grandsire, to his full brother if he has one of equal excellence, to his best son or best grandson. In such a fashion we compound the genes of this grandsire, and hope to obtain some puppies with his excellences intensified.

The best name in the pedigree may be some other dog or bitch, in which case it is his or her germ plasm that is to be doubled to serve for the foundation of the pedigrees of the puppies of the projected litter.

In making a mating, it is never wise to employ two dogs with the same positive fault. It is wise to use two dogs with as many of the same positive virtues as it is possible to obtain. Neither should faults balance each other, as one with a front too wide, the other with a front too narrow; one with a sway back, the other roach backed. Rather, one member of the mating should be right where the other is wrong. We cannot trust to obtain the intermediate, if we overcompensate the fault of one mate with a fault of the other.

NEGOTIATIONS TO USE THE STUD DOG

Plans to use a stud dog should be laid far enough in advance to enable one to make sure that the services of the dog will be available when they are required. Most men with a dog at public stud publish "stud cards," on which are printed the dog's pedigree and pertinent data pertaining to its record. These should be requested for all the dogs one contemplates using. Most such owners reserve the right to refuse to breed their dogs to bitches they deem unsuitable for them; they wish to safeguard their dog's reputation as a producer of superior puppies, by choosing the bitches to which he shall be bred. Therefore, it is advisable to submit a description of the bitch, with or without a picture of her, and her pedigree to the stud dog's owner at the time the application to use him is made.

Notification should be sent to the owner of the dog as soon as the bitch begins to show in heat, and she should be taken or sent by air or by railway express to the dog's owner about the time she is first recognized to be in full heat and ready to breed. The stud dog's owner should be advised by telegram or telephone just how she has been sent and just when she may be expected, and instruction should be given about how she is to be returned.

Extreme care should be used in securely crating a bitch for shipment when she is in heat. Such bitches are prone to chew their way out of insecure boxes and escape to be bred by some vagrant mongrel. A card containing a statement of the bitch's condition should be attached to the crate as a warning to the carrier to assure her greater security.

MATING

The only time the bitch may become pregnant is during her period of oestruation, a time also variously referred to as the "oestrus," "the season," and as being in "heat." A bitch's first season usually occurs when she is between six and nine months of age, with the average age being eight months. In rare instances it may occur as early as five months or as late as thirteen months of age. After the first season, oestrus usually recurs at intervals of approximately six months, though this too is subject to variation. Also, the bitch's cycle may be influenced by factors such as a change of environment or a change of climate, and her cycle will, of course, be changed if it is interrupted by pregnancy. Most bitches again come in season four to six months after whelping.

There is a decided controversy among breeders as to the wisdom of breeding a bitch during her first season. Some believe a really fine bitch should be bred during her first season in order that she may produce as many puppies as possible during the fertile years of her life span. Others feel that definite physical harm results from breeding a bitch at her first season. Since a normal healthy bitch can safely produce puppies until she is about nine years old, she can comfortably yield eight to ten litters with rests between them in her life. Any breeder should be satisfied with this production from one animal. It seems wiser, therefore, to avoid the risk of any harm and pass her first season. Bitches vary in temperament and in the ages at which they reach sufficient maturity for motherhood and its responsibilities. As with the human animal, stability comes with age and a dam is much more likely to be a good mother if she is out of the puppy phase herself. If the bitch is of show quality, she might become a champion between her first and second heats if not bred.

Usually, oestruation continues for a period of approximately three weeks, but this too is subject to variation. Prior to the beginning of the oestrus, there may be changes in the bitch's actions and demeanor; she may appear restless, or she may become increasingly affectionate. Often there is increased frequency of urination and the bitch may be inclined to lick her external parts. The breeder should be alert for any signs of the approach of oestrus since the bitch must be confined and protected at this time in order to preclude the possibility of the occurrence of a mating with any but the selected stud.

The first physical sign of oestrus is a bloody discharge of watery consistency. The mucous membrane lining the vulva becomes congested, enlarged, and reddened, and the external parts become puffy and swollen. The color of the discharge gradually deepens during the first day or two until it is a rich red color; then it gradually becomes lighter until by the tenth to twelfth day it has only a slightly reddish, or straw-colored, tinge. During the next day or so it becomes almost clear. During this same period, the swelling and hardness of the external parts gradually subside, and by the time the discharge has lost most of its color, the parts are softened and spongy. It is at this time that ovulation, the production of ripened ova (or eggs), takes place, although physical manifestations of oestrus may continue for another week.

A normal bitch has two ovaries which contain her ova. All the eggs she will produce during her lifetime are present in the ovaries at birth. Ordinarily, some of the ova ripen each time the bitch comes in season. Should a bitch fail to ovulate (produce ripened ova), she cannot, of course, become pregnant. Actually, only one ovary is necessary for ovulation, and loss of or damage to one ovary without impairment of the other will not prevent the bitch from producing puppies.

If fertilization does not occur, the ova (and this is also true of the sperm of the male) live only a short time—probably a couple of days at the most. Therefore, if mating takes place too long before or after ovulation, a bitch will not conceive, and the unfertilized ova will pass through the uterus into the vagina. Eventually they will either be absorbed or will pass out through the vulva by the same opening through which urination takes place. If fertilization does occur, the fertilized eggs become implanted on the inner surface of the uterus and grow to maturity.

Obviously, the breeder must exercise great care in determining when the dog and the bitch should be put together. Because the length of time between the beginning of the oestrus and the time of ovulation varies in different bitches, no hard and fast rule can be established, although the twelfth to fourteenth day is in most cases the correct time. The wise breeder will keep a daily record of the changes in the bitch's condition and will arrange to put the bitch and dog together when the discharge has become almost clear and the external parts are softened and spongy. If the bitch refuses the advances of the dog, it is preferable to separate the two, wait a day, then again permit the dog to approach the bitch.

Ordinarily, if the bitch is willing to accept the dog, fertilization of the ovum will take place. Usually one good service is sufficient, although two at intervals of twenty-four to forty-eight hours are often allowed.

Male dogs have glands on the penis which swell after passing the sphincter muscle of the vagina and "tie" the two animals together. The time may last for a period of a few minutes, a half hour, or occasionally up to an hour or more, but will end naturally when the locking glands have deflated the needful amount. While tying may increase the probability of success, in many cases no tie occurs, yet the bitches become pregnant.

Sperm are produced in the dog's testicles and are stored in the epididymis, a twisting tube at the side of the testicle. The occasional male dog whose testicles are not descended (a cryptorchid) is generally conceded to be sterile, although in a few instances it has been asserted that cryptorchids were capable of begetting progeny. The sterility in cryptorchids is believed to be due to the fact that the sperm are destroyed if the testicle remains within the abdominal cavity because the temperature is much higher there than in the normally descended testicle. Thus all sperm produced by the dog may be destroyed if both testicles are undescended. A monorchid (a dog with one testicle descended, the other undescended) may be fertile. Nevertheless, it is unwise to use a monorchid for stud purposes, because monorchidism is believed to be a heritable trait, and the monorchid, as well as the cryptorchid, is ineligible for the show ring.

After breeding, a bitch should be confined for a week to ten days to avoid mismating with another dog.

THE PREGNANCY AND WHELPING
OF THE BITCH

The "period of gestation" of the bitch, by which is meant the duration of her pregnancy, is usually estimated at sixty-three days. Many bitches, especially young ones, have their puppies as early as sixty days after they are bred. Cases have occurred in which strong puppies were born after only fifty-seven days, and there have been cases that required as many as sixty-six days. However, if puppies do not arrive by the sixty-fourth day, it is time to consult a veterinarian.

For the first five to six weeks of her pregnancy, the bitch requires no more than normal good care and unrestricted exercise. For that period, she needs no additional quantity of food, although her diet must contain sufficient amounts of all the food factors, as is stated in the division of this book that pertains to food. After the fifth to sixth week, the ration must be increased and the violence of exercise restricted. Normal running and walking are likely to be better for the pregnant bitch than a sedentary existence but she should not be permitted to jump, hunt, or fight during the latter half of her gestation. Violent activity may cause her to abort her puppies.

About a week before she is due to whelp, a bed should be prepared for her and she be persuaded to use it for sleeping. This bed may be a box of generous size, big enough to accommodate her with room for activity. It should be high enough to permit her to stand upright, and is better for having a hinged cover. An opening in one side will afford her ingress and egress. This box should be placed in a secluded location, away from any possible molestation by other dogs, animals, or children. The bitch must be made confident of her security in her box.

A few hours, or perhaps a day or two, before her whelping, the bitch will probably begin arranging the bedding of the box to suit herself, tearing blankets or cushions and nosing the parts into the corners. Before the whelping actually starts, however, it is best to substitute burlap sacking, securely tacked to the floor of the box. This is to provide traction for the puppies to reach the dam's breast.

The whelping may take place at night without any assistance from the owner. The box may be opened in the morning to reveal

WHELPING CALENDAR

Find the month and date on which your bitch was bred in one of the left-hand columns. Directly opposite that date, in the right-hand column, is her expected date of whelping, bearing in mind that 61 days is as common as 63.

Date bred	Date due to whelp	Date bred	Date due to whelp	Date bred	Date due to whelp	Date bred	Date due to whelp	Date bred	Date due to whelp	Date bred	Date due to whelp	Date bred	Date due to whelp	Date bred	Date due to whelp	Date bred	Date due to whelp	Date bred	Date due to whelp	Date bred	Date due to whelp	Date bred	Date due to whelp
January	March	February	April	March	May	April	June	May	July	June	August	July	September	August	October	September	November	October	December	November	January	December	February
1	5	1	5	1	3	1	3	1	3	1	3	1	2	1	3	1	3	1	3	1	3	1	2
2	6	2	6	2	4	2	4	2	4	2	4	2	3	2	4	2	4	2	4	2	4	2	3
3	7	3	7	3	5	3	5	3	5	3	5	3	4	3	5	3	5	3	5	3	5	3	4
4	8	4	8	4	6	4	6	4	6	4	6	4	5	4	6	4	6	4	6	4	6	4	5
5	9	5	9	5	7	5	7	5	7	5	7	5	6	5	7	5	7	5	7	5	7	5	6
6	10	6	10	6	8	6	8	6	8	6	8	6	7	6	8	6	8	6	8	6	8	6	7
7	11	7	11	7	9	7	9	7	9	7	9	7	8	7	9	7	9	7	9	7	9	7	8
8	12	8	12	8	10	8	10	8	10	8	10	8	9	8	10	8	10	8	10	8	10	8	9
9	13	9	13	9	11	9	11	9	11	9	11	9	10	9	11	9	11	9	11	9	11	9	10
10	14	10	14	10	12	10	12	10	12	10	12	10	11	10	12	10	12	10	12	10	12	10	11
11	15	11	15	11	13	11	13	11	13	11	13	11	12	11	13	11	13	11	13	11	13	11	12
12	16	12	16	12	14	12	14	12	14	12	14	12	13	12	14	12	14	12	14	12	14	12	13
13	17	13	17	13	15	13	15	13	15	13	15	13	14	13	15	13	15	13	15	13	15	13	14
14	18	14	18	14	16	14	16	14	16	14	16	14	15	14	16	14	16	14	16	14	16	14	15
15	19	15	19	15	17	15	17	15	17	15	17	15	16	15	17	15	17	15	17	15	17	15	16
16	20	16	20	16	18	16	18	16	18	16	18	16	17	16	18	16	18	16	18	16	18	16	17
17	21	17	21	17	19	17	19	17	19	17	19	17	18	17	19	17	19	17	19	17	19	17	18
18	22	18	22	18	20	18	20	18	20	18	20	18	19	18	20	18	20	18	20	18	20	18	19
19	23	19	23	19	21	19	21	19	21	19	21	19	20	19	21	19	21	19	21	19	21	19	20
20	24	20	24	20	22	20	22	20	22	20	22	20	21	20	22	20	22	20	22	20	22	20	21
21	25	21	25	21	23	21	23	21	23	21	23	21	22	21	23	21	23	21	23	21	23	21	22
22	26	22	26	22	24	22	24	22	24	22	24	22	23	22	24	22	24	22	24	22	24	22	23
23	27	23	27	23	25	23	25	23	25	23	25	23	24	23	25	23	25	23	25	23	25	23	24
24	28	24	28	24	26	24	26	24	26	24	26	24	25	24	26	24	26	24	26	24	26	24	25
25	29	25	29	25	27	25	27	25	27	25	27	25	26	25	27	25	27	25	27	25	27	25	26
26	30	26	30	26	28	26	28	26	28	26	28	26	27	26	28	26	28	26	28	26	28	26	27
27	31	27	May 1	27	29	27	29	27	29	27	29	27	28	27	29	27	29	27	29	27	29	27	28
28	Apr. 1	28	2	28	30	28	30	28	30	28	30	28	29	28	30	28	30	28	30	28	30	28	Mar. 1
29	2			29	31	29	July 1	29	31	29	31	29	30	29	31	29	Dec. 1	29	31	29	31	29	2
30	3			30	June 1	30	2	30	Aug. 1	30	Sep. 1	30	Oct. 1	30	Nov. 1	30	2	30	Jan. 1	30	Feb. 1	30	3
31	4			31	2			31	2			31	2	31	2			31	2			31	4

the happy bitch nursing a litter of complacent puppies. But she may need some assistance in her parturition. If whelping is recognized to be in process, it is best to help the bitch.

As the puppies arrive, one by one, the enveloping membranes should be removed as quickly as possible, lest the puppies suffocate. Having removed the membrane, the umbilical cord should be severed with clean scissors some three or four inches from the puppy's belly. (The part of the cord attached to the belly will dry up and drop off in a few days.) There is no need for any medicament or dressing of the cord after it is cut.

The bitch should be permitted to eat the afterbirth if she so desires, and she normally does. If she has no assistance, she will probably remove the membrane and sever the cord with her teeth. The only dangers are that she may delay too long or may bite the cord too short. Some bitches, few of them, eat their newborn puppies (especially bitches not adequately fed during pregnancy). This unlikelihood should be guarded against.

As they arrive, it is wise to remove all the puppies except one, placing them in a box or basket lined and covered by a woolen cloth, somewhere aside or away from the whelping bed, until all have come and the bitch's activity has ceased. The purpose of this is to prevent her from walking or lying on the whelps, and to keep her from being disturbed by the puppies' whining. A single puppy should be left with the bitch to ease her anxiety.

It is best that the "midwife" be somebody with whom the bitch is on intimate terms and in whom she has confidence. Some bitches exhibit a jealous fear and even viciousness while they are whelping. Such animals are few, and most appear grateful for gentle assistance through their ordeal.

The puppies arrive at intervals of a few minutes to an hour until all are delivered. It is wise to call a veterinarian if the interval is greater than one hour. Though such service is seldom needed, an experienced veterinarian can usually be depended upon to withdraw with obstetrical forceps an abnormally presented puppy. It is possible, but unlikely, that the veterinarian will recommend a Caesarian section. This surgery in the dog is not very grave, but it should be performed only by an expert veterinarian. It is unnecessary to describe the process here, or the subsequent management of the patient, since, if a Caesarian section should be necessary, the veterinarian will provide all the needed instructions.

Some bitches, at or immediately after their whelping period, go into a convulsive paralysis, which is called *eclampsia*. This is unlikely if the bitch throughout her pregnancy has had an adequate measure of calcium in her rations. The remedy for eclampsia is the intravenous or intramuscular administration of parenteral calcium. The bitch suspected of having eclampsia should be attended by a veterinarian.

Assuming that the whelping has been normal and without untoward incident, all of the puppies are returned to the bitch, and put, one by one, to the breast, which strong puppies will accept with alacrity. The less handling of puppies for the first four or five hours of their lives, the better. However, the litter should be looked over carefully for possible defectives and discards, which should be destroyed as soon as possible. There is no virtue in rearing hare-lipped, crippled, or mismarked puppies.

It is usually unwise to destroy sound, healthy puppies just to reduce the number in the litter, since it is impossible to sort young puppies for excellence and one may be destroying the best member of the litter, a future champion. Unless a litter is extraordinarily numerous, the dam, if well fed, can probably suckle them all. If it is found that her milk is insufficient, the litter may be artificially fed or may be divided, and the surplus placed on a foster mother if it is possible to obtain one. The foster mother need not be of the same breed as the puppies, a mongrel being as good as any. She should be approximately the same size as the actual mother of the puppies, clean, healthy, and her other puppies should be of as nearly the same age as the ones she is to take over as possible. She should be removed from her own puppies (which may well be destroyed) and her breasts be permitted to fill with milk until she is somewhat uncomfortable, at which time her foster puppies can be put to her breasts and will usually be accepted without difficulty. Unless the services of the foster mother are really required, it is better not to use her.

The whelping bitch may be grateful for a warm meal even between the arrivals of her puppies. As soon as her chore is over, she should be offered food in her box. This should be of cereal and milk or of meat and broth, something sloppy. She will probably not leave her puppies to eat and her meals must be brought to her.

It is wise to give a mild laxative for her bowels, also milk of magnesia. She will be reluctant to get out of her box even to relieve herself for about two days, but she should be urged, even forced, to do so regularly. A sensible bitch will soon settle down to care for her brood and will seldom give further trouble. She should be fed often and well, all that she can be induced to eat during her entire lactation.

As a preventive for infections sometimes occurring after whelping, some experienced breeders and veterinarians recommend injecting the bitch with penicillin or another antibiotic immediately following the birth of the last puppy. Oral doses of the same drug may be given daily thereafter for the first week. It is best to consult your veterinarian about this treatment.

18

Good Dog Keeping Practices

Pride of ownership is greatly enhanced when the owner takes care to maintain his dog in the best possible condition at all times. And meticulous grooming not only will make the dog look better but also will make him feel better. As part of the regular, daily routine, the grooming of the dog will prove neither arduous nor time consuming; it will also obviate the necessity for indulging in a rigorous program designed to correct the unkempt state in which too many owners permit their dogs to appear. Certainly, spending a few minutes each day will be well worth while, for the result will be a healthier, happier, and more desirable canine companion.

THAT DOGGY ODOR

Many persons are disgusted to the point of refusal to keep a dog by what they fancy is a "doggy odor." Of course, almost everything has a characteristic odor—everyone is familiar with the smell of the rose. No one would want the dog to smell like a rose, and, conversely, the world wouldn't like it very well if the rose smelled doggy. The dog must emit a certain amount of characteristic odor or he woudn't be a dog. That seems to be his God-given grant. However, when the odor becomes too strong and obnoxious, then it is time to look for the reason. In most cases it is the result of clogged anal glands. If this be the case, all one must do to rid the pet of his odor is to express the contents of these glands and apply to the anal region a little soap and water.

If the odor is one of putrefaction, look to his mouth for the trouble. The teeth may need scaling, or a diseased root of some one or two teeth that need to be treated may be the source of the odor. In some dogs there is a fold or a crease in the lower lip near the lower canine tooth, and this may need attention. This spot is favored by fungi that cause considerable damage to the part. The smell here is somewhat akin to the odor of human feet that have been attacked by the fungus of athlete's foot.

The odor may be coming from the coat if the dog is heavily infested with fleas or lice. Too, dogs seem to enjoy the odor of dead fish and often roll on a foul smelling fish that has been cast up on the beach. The dog with a bad case of otitis can fairly "drive you out of the room" with this peculiar odor. Obviously, the way to rid the dog of odor is to find from whence it comes and then take steps to eliminate it. Some dogs have a tendency toward excessive flatulence (gas). These animals should have a complete change of diet and with the reducing of the carbohydrate content, a teaspoon of granular charcoal should be added to each feeding.

BATHING THE DOG

There is little to say about giving a bath to a dog, except that he shall be placed in a tub of warm (not hot) water and thoroughly scrubbed. He may, like a spoiled child, object to the ordeal, but if handled gently and firmly he will submit to what he knows to be inevitable.

The water must be only tepid, so as not to shock or chill the dog. A bland, unmedicated soap is best, for such soaps do not irritate the skin or dry out the hair. Even better than soap is one of the powdered detergents marketed especially for this purpose. They rinse away better and more easily than soap and do not leave the coat gummy or sticky.

It is best to begin with the face, which should be thoroughly and briskly washed with a cloth. Care should be taken that the cleaning solvent does not get into the dog's eyes, not because of the likelihood of causing permanent harm, but because such an experience is unpleasant to the dog and prone to prejudice him against future baths. The interior of the ear canals should be thoroughly cleansed until they not only look clean but also until no unpleasant odor comes from them. The head may then be rinsed and dried before proceeding to the body. Especial attention should be given to the drying of the ears, inside and outside. Many ear infections arise from failure to dry the canals completely.

With the head bathed and the surplus water removed from that part, the body must be soaked thoroughly with water, either with a hose or by dipping the water from the bath and pouring it over the dog's back until he is totally wetted. Thereafter, the soap or detergent should be applied and rubbed until it lathers freely. A stiff brush is useful in penetrating the coat and cleansing the skin. It is not sufficient to wash only the back and sides—the belly, neck, legs, feet, and tail must all be scrubbed thoroughly.

If the dog is very dirty, it may be well to rinse him lightly and repeat the soaping process and scrub again. Thereafter, the dog must be rinsed with warm (tepid) water until all suds and soil come away. If a bath spray is available, the rinsing is an easy matter. If the dog must be rinsed in standing water, it will be needful to renew it two or three times.

When he is thoroughly rinsed, it is well to remove such surplus water as may be squeezed with the hand, after which he is enveloped with a turkish towel, lifted from the tub, and rubbed until he is dry. This will probably require two or three dry towels. In the process of drying the dog, it is well to return again and again to the interior of the ears.

THE DOG'S TEETH

The dog, like the human being, has two successive sets of teeth, the so-called milk teeth or baby teeth, which are shed and replaced later by the permanent teeth. The temporary teeth, which begin to emerge when the puppy is two and a half to three weeks of age, offer no difficulty. The full set of milk teeth (consisting usually of six incisors and two canines in each jaw, with four molars in the upper jaw and six molars in the lower jaw) is completed usually just before weaning time. Except for some obvious malformation, the milk teeth may be ignored and forgotten about.

At about the fourth month the baby teeth are shed and gradually replaced by the permanent teeth. This shedding and replacement

252

process may consume some three or four months. This is about the most critical period of the dog's life—his adolescence. Some constitutionally vigorous dogs go through their teething easily, with no seeming awareness that the change is taking place. Others, less vigorous, may suffer from soreness of the gums, go off in flesh, and require pampering. While they are teething, puppies should be particularly protected from exposure to infectious diseases and should be fed on nutritious foods, especially meat and milk.

The permanent teeth normally consist of 42—six incisors and two canines (fangs) in each jaw, with twelve molars in the upper jaw and fourteen in the lower jaw. Occasionally the front molars fail to emerge; this deficiency is considered by most judges to be only a minor fault, if the absence is noticed at all.

Dentition is a heritable factor in the dog, and some dogs have soft, brittle and defective permanent teeth, no matter how excellent the diet and the care given them. The teeth of those dogs which are predisposed to have excellent sound ones, however, can be ruined by an inferior diet prior to and during the period of their eruption. At this time, for the teeth to develop properly, a dog must have an adequate supply of calcium phosphate and vitamin D, besides all the protein he can consume.

Often the permanent teeth emerge before the shedding of the milk teeth, in which case the dog may have parts of both sets at the same time. The milk teeth will eventually drop out, but as long as they remain they may deflect or displace the second teeth in the process of their growth. The incisors are the teeth in which a malformation may result from the late dropping of the baby teeth. When it is realized just how important a correct "bite" may be deemed in the show ring, the hazards of permitting the baby teeth to deflect the permanent set will be understood.

The baby teeth in such a case must be dislodged and removed. The roots of the baby teeth are resorbed in the gums, and the teeth can usually be extracted by firm pressure of thumb and finger, although it may be necessary to employ forceps or to take the puppy to the veterinarian.

The permanent teeth of the puppy are usually somewhat overshot, by which is meant that the upper incisors protrude over and do not play upon the lower incisors. Maturity may be trusted to remedy this apparent defect unless it is too pronounced.

An undershot mouth in a puppy, on the other hand, tends to grow worse as the dog matures. Whether or not it has been caused by the displacement of the permanent teeth by the persistence of the milk teeth, it can sometimes be remedied (or at least bettered) by frequent hard pressure of the thumb on the lower jaw, forcing the lower teeth backward to meet the upper ones. Braces on dog teeth have seldom proved efficacious, but pressure and massage are worth trying on the bad mouth of an otherwise excellent puppy.

High and persistent fevers, especially from the fourth to the ninth month, sometimes result in discolored, pitted, and defective teeth, commonly called "distemper teeth." They often result from maladies other than distemper. There is little that can be done for them. They are unpleasant to see and are subject to penalty in the show ring, but are serviceable to the dog. Distemper teeth are not in themselves heritable, but the predisposition for their development appears to be. At least, at the teething age, the offspring from distemper toothed ancestors seem to be especially prone to fevers which impair their dentition.

Older dogs, especially those fed largely upon carbohydrates, tend to accumulate more or less tartar upon their teeth. The tartar generally starts at the gum line on the molars and extends gradually to the cusp. To rectify this condition, the dog's teeth should be scaled by a veterinarian.

The cleanliness of a dog's mouth may be brought about and the formation of tartar discouraged by the scouring of the teeth with a moist cloth dipped in a mixture of equal parts of table salt and baking soda.

A large bone given the dog to chew on or play with tends to prevent tartar from forming on the teeth. If tartar is present, the chewing and gnawing on the bone will help to remove the deposit mechanically. A bone given to puppies will act as a teething ring and aid in the cutting of the permanent teeth. So will beef hide strips you can buy in pet shops.

CARE OF THE NAILS

The nails of the dog should be kept shortened and blunted right down to the quick—never into the quick. If this is not done, the toes may spread and the foot may splay into a veritable pancake.

Some dogs have naturally flat feet, which they have inherited. No pretense is made that the shortening of the nails of such a foot will obviate the fault entirely and make the foot beautiful or serviceable.

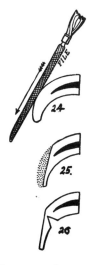

NAIL TRIMMING ILLUSTRATED

The method here illustrated is to take a sharp file and stroke the nail downwards in the direction of the arrow, as in Figure 24, until it assumes the shape in Figure 25, the shaded portion being the part removed, a three-cornered file should then be used on the underside just missing the quick, as in Figure 26, and the operation is then complete, the dog running about quickly wears the nail to the proper shape.

It will only improve the appearance and make the best of an obvious fault. Short nails do, however, emphasize the excellence of a good foot.

Some dogs keep their nails short by digging and friction. Their nails require little attention, but it is a rare dog whose foot cannot be bettered by artificially shortening the nails.

Nail clippers are available, made especially for the purpose. After using them, the sides of the nail should be filed away as much as is possible without touching the quick. Carefully done, it causes the dog no discomfort. But, once the quick of a dog's nail has been injured, he may forever afterward resent and fight having his feet treated or even having them examined.

The obvious horn of the nail can be removed, after which the quick will recede to permit the removal of more horn the following week. This process may be kept up until the nail is as short and blunt as it can be made, after which nails will need attention only at intervals of six weeks or two months.

BIBLIOGRAPHY

ALL OWNERS of pure-bred·dogs will benefit themselves and their dogs by enriching their knowledge of breeds and of canine care, training, breeding, psychology and other important aspects of dog management. The following list of books covers further reading recommended by judges, veterinarians, breeders, trainers and other authorities. Books may be obtained at the finer book stores and pet shops, or through Howell Book House Inc., publishers, New York.

Breed Books

AFGHAN HOUND, Complete	Miller & Gilbert
AIREDALE, New Complete	Edwards
ALASKAN MALAMUTE, Complete	Riddle & Seeley
BASSET HOUND, Complete	Braun
BEAGLE, Complete	Noted Authorities
BLOODHOUND, Complete	Brey & Reed
BOXER, Complete	Denlinger
BRITTANY SPANIEL, Complete	Riddle
BULLDOG, New Complete	Hanes
BULL TERRIER, New Complete	Eberhard
CAIRN TERRIER, Complete	Marvin
CHIHUAHUA, Complete	Noted Authorities
COCKER SPANIEL, New	Kraeuchi
COLLIE, Complete	Official Publication of the
Collie Club of America	
DACHSHUND, The New	Meistrell
DOBERMAN PINSCHER, New	Walker
ENGLISH SETTER, New Complete	Tuck & Howell
ENGLISH SPRINGER SPANIEL, New	
Goodall & Gasow	
FOX TERRIER, New Complete	Silvernail
GERMAN SHEPHERD DOG, Complete	Bennett
GERMAN SHORTHAIRED POINTER, New	Maxwell
GOLDEN RETRIEVER, Complete	Fischer
GREAT DANE, New Complete	Noted Authorities
GREAT PYRENEES, Complete	Strang & Giffin
IRISH SETTER, New	Thompson
IRISH WOLFHOUND, Complete	Starbuck
KEESHOND, Complete	Peterson
LABRADOR RETRIEVER, Complete	Warwick
LHASA APSO, Complete	Herbel
MINIATURE SCHNAUZER, Complete	Eskrigge
NEWFOUNDLAND, New Complete	Chern
NORWEGIAN ELKHOUND, New Complete	Wallo
OLD ENGLISH SHEEPDOG, Complete	Mandeville
PEKINGESE, Quigley Book of	Quigley
PEMBROKE WELSH CORGI, Complete	
Sargent & Harper	
POMERANIAN, New Complete	Ricketts
POODLE, New Complete	Hopkins & Irick
POODLE CLIPPING AND GROOMING BOOK,	
Complete	Kalstone
PUG, Complete	Trullinger
PULI, Complete	Owen
ST. BERNARD, New Complete	
Noted Authorities, rev. Raulston	
SAMOYED, Complete	Ward
SCHIPPERKE, Official Book of	Root, Martin, Kent
SCOTTISH TERRIER, Complete	Marvin
SHETLAND SHEEPDOG, New	Riddle
SHIH TZU, The (English)	Dadds
SIBERIAN HUSKY, Complete	Demidoff
TERRIERS, The Book of All	Marvin
TOY DOGS, Kalstone Guide to Grooming All	
Kalstone	
TOY DOGS, All About	Ricketts
WEST HIGHLAND WHITE TERRIER,	
Complete	Marvin
WHIPPET, Complete	Pegram
YORKSHIRE TERRIER, Complete	
Gordon & Bennett	

Care and Training

DOG OBEDIENCE, Complete Book of	Saunders
NOVICE, OPEN AND UTILITY COURSES	
Saunders	
DOG CARE AND TRAINING, Howell	
Book of	Howell, Denlinger, Merrick
DOG CARE AND TRAINING FOR BOYS	
AND GIRLS	Saunders
DOG TRAINING FOR KIDS	Benjamin
DOG TRAINING, Koehler Method of	Koehler
GO FIND! Training Your Dog to Track	Davis
GUARD DOG TRAINING, Koehler Method of	
Koehler	
OPEN OBEDIENCE FOR RING, HOME	
AND FIELD, Koehler Method of	Koehler
SPANIELS FOR SPORT (English)	Radcliffe
SUCCESSFUL DOG TRAINING, The	
Pearsall Guide to	Pearsall
TRAIN YOUR OWN GUN DOG,	
How to	Goodall
TRAINING THE RETRIEVER	Kersley
TRAINING YOUR DOG TO WIN	
OBEDIENCE TITLES	Morsell
UTILITY DOG TRAINING, Koehler Method of	
Koehler	

Breeding

ART OF BREEDING BETTER DOGS, New	Onstott
HOW TO BREED DOGS	Whitney
HOW PUPPIES ARE BORN	Prine
INHERITANCE OF COAT COLOR	
IN DOGS	Little

General

COMPLETE DOG BOOK, The	
Official Pub. of American Kennel Club	
DISNEY ANIMALS, World of	Koehler
DOG IN ACTION, The	Lyon
DOG BEHAVIOR, New Knowledge of	
Pfaffenberger	
DOG JUDGING, Nicholas Guide to	Nicholas
DOG NUTRITION, Collins Guide to	Collins
DOG PEOPLE ARE CRAZY	Riddle
DOG PSYCHOLOGY	Whitney
DOG STANDARDS ILLUSTRATED	
DOGSTEPS, Illustrated Gait at a Glance	Elliott
ENCYCLOPEDIA OF DOGS, International	
Dangerfield, Howell & Riddle	
JUNIOR SHOWMANSHIP HANDBOOK	
Brown & Mason	
MY TIMES WITH DOGS	Fletcher
RICHES TO BITCHES	Shattuck
SUCCESSFUL DOG SHOWING, Forsyth Guide to	
Forsyth	
TRIM, GROOM AND SHOW YOUR DOG,	
How to	Saunders
WHY DOES YOUR DOG DO THAT?	Bergman
WILD DOGS in Life and Legend	Riddle
WORLD OF SLED DOGS, From Siberia to	
Sport Racing	Coppinger
OUR PUPPY'S BABY BOOK (blue or pink)	